Cities of Art

Cities of Art

Milan

Edited by
Roberta D'Adda
Massimo Zanella

Editor
Valerio Terraroli

Design
Marcello Francone

Editorial Coordination
Eva Vanzella

Copy Editing
Leandra R. Parker, Doriana Comerlati

Layout
Massimo Zanella

Translations
Paul Metcalfe for *Scriptum*, Rome

Iconographical Research
Paola Lamanna, Massimo Zanella

City Map
Studio Margil, Certosa di Pavia

First published in Italy in 2015 by
Skira Editore S.p.A.
Palazzo Casati Stampa
via Torino 61
20123 Milano, Italy
www.skira.net

Printed and bound in Italy. First edition

*Itineraries 3 and 8 have been conceived
by Maria Vittoria Capitanucci*

Crediti fotografici
Archivio Fondazione Arnaldo Pomodoro
Archivio Scala, Firenze
© Atlantide Phototravel/Corbis
© Carlo Cerchioli/Grazia Neri
DeAgostini Picture Library/Scala, Firenze
Enrico Formica, Milano
Enrico Magri Studio, Milano
Andrea Melzi, Milano
© Marcello Mencarini/Grazia Neri
Paolo Manusardi, Milano
Grazia Neri
Mauro Ranzani
Foto Saporetti/Roberto Mascaroni
Foto Sime/Franco Cogoli
Foto Sime/Luca De Ros
Foto Sime/Kaos03
Foto Sime/Massimo Ripani
Sime, Milano
Saverio Lombardi Vallauri
Leo Torri
Fototeca Veneranda Fabbrica del Duomo

Contents

Introduction

A city of business, fashion and design, an industrial and administrative centre, the goal for generations of Italian immigrants and daily destination of thousands of commuters, home to publishers, newspapers and television networks, richly provided with theatres, museums, galleries and universities, Milan in the 21st century is a metropolis that preserves the symbols of a long and illustrious past while displaying its capacity for change and renewal.

Milan is the hub of a highly urbanised territorial system that dominates the entire central and western area of Lombardy. While the city's outskirts were subjected during the 20th century to large-scale speculative building that today raises complex problems of conversion and redevelopment, the map of the historical centre was instead almost entirely redrawn between the end of the 19th century and the years after World War I. Wholesale urban clearance, rebuilding and radical restructuring of the road system have given Milan a distinctive character with respect to the other Italian cities endowed with a great artistic heritage. The landmarks of an illustrious past emerge within a heterogeneous but unquestionably rich and stimulating urban fabric: from the later stages of the Roman empire to the age of the city-states, from the Visconti and Sforza dynasties to the era of Spanish regime, from Habsburg rule in the 18th century to the Napoleonic splendours, from the initial phases of industrialisation to Art Nouveau and Deco, all the way to the postwar period and the contemporary world.

The city has a radial layout with a series of main roads branching out like spokes from the immediately identifiable hub of the Cathedral Square toward the old city gates and then on into the outlying areas. This type of structure is characteristic of cities developed in successive phases over a long period of time within concentric rings of defensive walls. The first of these in Milan dates from the 1st century BC, during the Roman era. Initially equipped with four main gates and stretching for about 3.5 kilometres, the walls were expanded slightly during the imperial era, when *Mediolanum* (the ancient Roman name of Milan) became the residence of one of the emperors of the West. It was in the 12th century, when Milan was a city-state, that the suburban areas known as *borghi*, developed along the roads radiating out from the old gates (hence the names Via Borgonuovo and Via Borgospesso, for example), were encompassed within a perimeter stretching over 6 kilometres. The initial structure of embankments fortified with stakes and surrounded by a moat was gradually replaced with a ring of walls with battlements, which was completed in the 14th century. The medieval walls had six fortified main gates consisting of two arches flanked by towers (those of the Porta Nuova in Via Manzoni being still visible today) and other smaller postern gates. The system of the eight main roads leading to the city gates from the centre of political power (Piazza del Broletto, today Piazza dei Mercanti, adjacent to Piazza del Duomo, the Cathedral Square) was also reshaped in the era of the city-state.

The Spanish governor Ferrante Gonzaga ordered the construction of new city walls toward the end of the 16th century, maintaining the same centre and expanding the old circuit to a total perimeter of over 11 kilometres. There were twelve gates, built as projections of their medieval counterparts. The built-up areas inside the walls were, however, limited and alternated in the peripheral sections with parks, vegetable gardens and cultivated fields. These walls lasted until the end of the 18th century, when, during the age of French domination, it was decided to demolish the medieval gates and create a broad tree-lined ring road on the fortifications, some traces of which still survive in the area of Porta Venezia. The decision to knock down the walls was finally taken with the city's first urban planning scheme (1884–1885). A process of expansion had in any case begun halfway through the 19th century that was to change the shape, size and structure of Milan completely. This involved both the absorption of the suburbs outside the walls and the construction – often uncontrolled and wholly unregulated until the 1960s – of huge residential districts, mostly of mediocre urban quality, and vast decentralised industrial areas, located above all to the north.

In the Roman era, the centre of Milan was the forum, located on the place where the Biblioteca Ambrosiana (Ambrosian Library) stands today. The city had a theatre (remains of which can still be seen in the basement of the stock exchange), a circus (stretches of wall in Via Circo), an amphitheatre (large sections of foundations unearthed in Via Arena) and an imperial palace (situated in the Carrobbio area). One of the polygonal towers forming part of the walls in the imperial age still stands intact in the courtyard of the Archaeological Museum. The ancient city's perpendicular grid of roads can still be seen in the Cordusio area. Milan was a key centre for the nascent Christian religion in late antiquity. It was here that Constantine issued the celebrated edict of tolerance in 313 and here that an illustrious and lasting tradition commenced with Saint Ambrose's reign as bishop in 374. The numerous churches built (mostly outside the walls) and subsequently renovated or destroyed include the *basilica maior* of Santa Tecla with the adjoining Baptistery of San Giovanni alle Fonti (on the site of the present cathedral) and the still existing Basilicas of San Nazaro Maggiore, Sant'Ambrogio and San Simpliciano.

The most significant traces of the era of the city-state are to be found in the Romanesque structure of Sant'Ambrogio, the Palazzo della Ragione (or Broletto) and the Shrine of San Satiro. While many churches were demolished between the 18th and 20th centuries, the medieval appearance of numerous other ecclesiastical buildings is the result of 19th-century restoration largely based on an interpretive approach. A crucial impact was made on the city's structure by the rule of Gian Galeazzo Visconti, who secured Milan's elevation to the status of a duchy in 1395. He ordered the construction of a new cathedral in the late Gothic style and decided to move the ducal palace from the vicinity of the cathedral to a new fortified area on the northwest edge of the residential section, thus paving the way for the present-day castle. It was in this period that the Ospedale Maggiore and the Lazzaretto were built and the network of canals (known as the *navigli*) began to take shape. The city had in fact already been equipped in Roman times with a complex system to channel water from the Nirone, Seveso, Olona (or Vetra), Ticino and Adda rivers, initially for defensive purpose and then in order to meet the needs of inhabitants and artisans as well as facilitating the transport of goods and provisions. It was midway through the 15th century that a system of locks was developed enabling vessels to move between canals at different levels. Those involved in the project included Leonardo da Vinci. The system of canals, almost entirely paved over during the 19th and 20th centuries, was completed with a series of docks for unloading. (Those constructed at Porta Ticinese in the 17th century are still visible.)

During the initial phase of Spanish rule, the activities of Carlo and Federico Borromeo, bishops of Sant'Ambrogio respectively during the periods 1560–1584 and 1595–1631, involved some important innovations also in architectural terms, starting with initiatives linked to the Counter-Reformation. The ecclesiastical structures were reorganised, numerous charitable institutes were created, colleges were set up to train new members of the clergy, and the Biblioteca Ambrosiana was founded in 1609 as a library open to the public. Having taken over from the Spanish in the 18th century, the Austrians embarked in the age of Charles VI and Maria Theresa on a series of reforms with support from active and intelligent officials.

Spurred on by the enlightened intellectuals who wrote in the journal *Il Caffè*, the city witnessed the founding of institutions such as the Patriotic Society for the Development of Science, Technology and Economics and the Brera Academy and Library. The person primarily responsible for urban modernisation was the architect Giuseppe Piermarini, whose works included numerous stately mansions, the conversion of many religious buildings into public offices after the Habsburg confiscation of church property, the building of new piazzas and the creation of public gardens in the area of Porta Venezia.

With the arrival of Napoleon, Milan became the capital of the Cisalpine Republic (then the Italian Republic and finally the Kingdom of Italy as from 1805) and huge, ambitious projects were launched at the beginning of the new century to meet the need for urban structures capable of coping with the growing population and to bring the city into line with a new vision of public space. Only some of these were actually put into effect. The fortifications around the Castle were demolished so as to free the vast area they occupied, known as the Foro Buonaparte, for non-military use and the Corso Sempione, the new highway for France, was thus grafted onto the fabric of the historical city. While Giovanni Antonio Antolini's plans for an immense complex of public buildings, offices, markets and theatres in this area were only partially put into effect, they were taken into account in 1807, when the committee of public works published a new plan to reorganise the road system, which involved among other things the widening and realignment of some streets (with the associated demolition work). With the Restoration, strong population growth was accompanied by large-scale activity in the construction sector, with the accentuated occupation of open spaces and constant renovation and improvement of old buildings. The face of the city changed considerably in the space of a few decades. While the elegant buildings were concentrated in the northeast part of the city, which was more salubrious and less built-up, with wide roads and large gardens, the southern districts such as Porta Romana became largely lower-class neighbourhoods.

The increase in population was instead accompanied in the final decades of the 19th century by a decrease in the number of residential buildings as the old low-density constructions were replaced with new intensive types. While new districts were created, there were projects to redevelop existing built-up areas such as the Lazzaretto, which was entirely demolished, and the complex of the Sforza Castle, which was the object of attempted speculation. The city centre was modernised, not least in connection with the new celebratory requirements of the newly unified state. The Cathedral Square was rebuilt on a monumental scale, the Vittorio Emanuele II Gallery was created at the cost of destroying an entire neighbourhood, and other buildings were demolished in order to create Via Dante as a new thoroughfare connecting the Cathedral and the Castle. These were, however, also years of restoration work on churches, piazzas and city gates attesting to renewed interest in monuments capable of bearing witness to the national genius. The medieval face of Milan was thus 'recreated' as it can still be seen today in the Castle and, for example, in the Churches of Sant'Eustorgio, San Simpliciano, San Celso and Santa Maria del Carmine.

The drafting of the city's first planning scheme in 1884 and its revision in 1885 (the Beruto plan) laid the foundations for what was to come over the next one hundred years. Housing and small and medium-sized firms were to be located in Milan, large industrial plants in the neighbouring municipalities, and administration and services in the area between Piazza della Scala, Piazza Cordusio and the Ambrosian Library. Radical projects were discontinued both for monumental structures and for reorganisation of the road system in the city inside the walls. Attempts were made to regulate the development of private building so as to ensure expansion on the basis of a regular grid of roads with no differentiation as to use.

The districts of Cordusio, Via Dante, Foro Buonaparte and Via XX Settembre came into being at the end of the 19th century together with the Sempione Park. The first four districts of public housing for the working class were created (Mac Mahon, Spaventa, Ripamonti and Ribaldi). Industrialisation on a massive scale led among other things to the founding of historic companies such as OM, Alfa Romeo, Breda, Marelli, Pirelli and Falck. While middle-class homes were characterised by Art Nouveau and eclecticism, blocks of flats predominated in working-class districts, detached houses with garden being comparatively rare.

Only a third of the land allocated for construction in the Beruto plan was actually built-up at the beginning of the 20th century, but the density in the new areas was three times the envisaged level and a great deal of recent building was on land not covered by the plan. The years of the Fascist regime saw great changes in the urban layout. The city's new planning scheme of 1934 envisaged a series of clearance and rebuilding projects for the central areas that would have led to the almost complete disappearance of historical buildings if carried out in full. The reorganisation of railway stations freed some central and western areas for quality building. While the centre of the city (Piazza Diaz, Piazza Affari, Piazza della Repubblica and Corso Matteotti) was increasingly given over to head offices, the local population was diverted toward the outskirts. The new architectural vocabularies of Art Deco and Rationalism informed all the most important works of public building: the district-level Fascist headquarters, the new Trade Fair Complex, the San Siro Stadium, the Palazzo dell'Arte (home of the Milan Triennale), the Law

Courts, the Seaplane Station, the Forlanini Airport, the Vigorelli Velodrome, the Niguarda Hospital, the new Polytechnic in the Città Studi area, the Milan University, the Catholic University and the new building for the Bocconi University.

The bombing of 1943 affected 25% of the city's homes, the railways and the large factories. The new urban planning scheme of 1953 envisaged a road system making it possible to drive cars into the historical centre (thus involving wholesale demolition in the area of Piazza San Babila, Piazza Missori, Piazza San Sepolcro and Via Vincenzo Monti) as well as the creation of a system of self-sufficient suburban residential districts and an underground railway. The plan paid insufficient attention to the city's historical and architectural heritage and failed to halt intense and uncontrolled expansion in the outskirts. The new phenomenon of skyscrapers made its appearance in the city, the best-known examples being the Pirelli and Velasca buildings.

A new phase began in the 1970s with a new focus on historical buildings and the quality of the urban environment accompanied by growing efforts to foster the presence in urban areas of lower-class housing and small firms as well as the improvement of public services. The decrease in population and the crisis affecting major sectors of production raised complex problems as regards the conversion and redevelopment of built-up areas not only in the historical centre but also and above all in the vast intermediate and peripheral areas created as from the end of the 19th century.

Today, the skyline of Milan has changed! Over the last decade, the city has undergone some considerable transformations, clearly visible both in the city centre and in what used to be referred to as its historic suburbs, that have now been transformed into areas of great charm and interest that form an integral part of the metropolis. Whether along the narrow streets of the city centre or along its busy avenues, the perception of old *Mediolanum* has changed completely. For decades the points of reference for visitors were the Madonnina (the gilded statue of the Virgin crowning the tallest spire of the Duomo), the Velasca Tower designed by the BBPR firm of architects, Gio Ponti's Pirelli skyscraper, the towers in the Stazione Centrale area (the city's first high-rise buildings), and Monte Rosa in the distance: but now these have been somewhat outdone by new, striking features – some invasive, others more pleasant or interesting, but always hyper-contemporary. Towering against the backdrop of Milan are new skyscrapers as well as many new structures that come across as being less 'over the top'. Here the horizontal development of office or residential buildings reflects what has long been a hallmark of Milanese architecture, a modern yet always restrained distinguishing feature. The city's access routes have also changed, and for the better. Within a typically metropolitan yet nondescript landscape – ring roads, popular housing estates of questionable quality from the 1960s-1980s, unimpressive office towers from the following decade, and industrial sheds – master plans are now being drawn to redefine old industrial areas through interesting architectural projects. Milan has expanded and come to incorporate adjacent municipalities, finally turning into 'Greater Milan'. This has occurred, for instance, with the Bicocca (formerly Pirelli) area along the route leading to Sesto San Giovanni, which has been completely redeveloped by Vittorio Gregotti, paving the way for the later work in the Portello and Maciachini districts as well as for CityLife and Porta Nuova.

Milan is also renewing itself through the events connected to Expo 2015, 'Feeding the Planet'. The site of the world fair in the north-west of the city features pavilions and new infrastructures intended to play a role even beyond the international event. In the same area other projects are being developed, such as the one for office spaces and commercial venues designed by De Lucchi, Chipperfield and Zucchi in the former Alfa Romeo industrial area, or the master plan by Citterio and Caputo for the conversion of the Cascina Merlata area into a multifunctional complex, with the involvement of a considerable number of leading professionals – including MAB, C+S, Zucchi, etc.

To the south, in the municipality of Assago, a new 'city gate' has been completed, on a master plan by the Dutch architect Erick van Egeraat, with experimental, sustainable projects by Zucchi, Park Associati, abda, and OBR. This development work was foreshadowed by the creation of two innovative gateways to Milan: the wonderful Deposito ATM Famagosta, designed by the master Vico Magistretti, and the nearby Collegio di Milano, designed by Marco Zanuso (with an extension currently being developed by Piuarch). Encompassing efforts to recompose the urban fabric, new residential buildings in former industrial areas and genuine master plans for areas which had never really been completed, a range of different itineraries are available for visitors wishing to explore the contemporary city. On this specific occasion, the choice has been made to identify and illustrate two major areas which have undergone profound transformation through wide-ranging redevelopment work, often entrusted to leading international architects. These macro-sectors of the city, of course, are also dotted with architectural traces from previous periods, such as 'small treasures' of Modernism ranging from the 1930s to the post-war period. While often overlooked, these highly experimental projects set the foundations for contemporary architecture, illustrating the work of leading figures such as Portaluppi, Ponti, Muzio, Terragni and Lingeri, followed by Gardella, Caccia Dominioni, Magistretti, BBPR, the Latis and Soncini brothers, Asnago and Vender.

From Piazza del Duomo to Corso Sempione:
The Religious and Civic Heart of the City

1

F ollowing the course of the great urban-planning projects that redesigned the northwest sector of the city on a monumental scale
between the end of the 18th century and the beginning of the 20th century, this itinerary includes two of the key places in Milan's history, namely the Cathedral and the Castle, the Duomo and the Castello Sforzesco,
ancient architectural settings for priceless treasures of art.

The present-day layout of **Piazza del Duomo**, the Cathedral Square and
symbolic heart of the city, took shape through urban clearance and construction as from the second half of the 19th century on the basis of a
project that came in for a great deal of criticism and was never entirely
completed. The vast area of the present-day piazza and the buildings lining its sides was occupied by the subsequently destroyed *basilica maior*
and the Ambrosian Baptistery of San Giovanni alle Fonti back in the
4th century. Irregular in shape and far smaller than at present, it fitted
harmoniously into the grid of the ancient Roman urban fabric in the
medieval era, and constituted the fulcrum of the city's religious and civic
life as the location of the two cathedrals of Santa Tecla and Santa Maria
Maggiore. Respectively referred to as the Summer and Winter Cathedrals in accordance with a custom widely adopted in the area of the Po
Valley, they each included a baptistery. The municipal authorities also
had their first official building, known as the Broletto Vecchio, in the
vicinity. The construction of the new cathedral, which began in 1386
and continued until the 19th century, provided the basis for a reshap-
ing of this space. The building was situated at an angle to the Roman
grid of roads and its colossal bulk paved the way for the subsequent monumental developments. The idea of redesigning the small square gathered momentum at the beginning of the 19th century and took shape
in 1876 with plans drawn up by the architect Giuseppe Mengoni for
the city council. Demolition on a massive scale would clear an enormous

Cathedral, façade

rectangular space to serve as the starting point for a series of major thoroughfares radiating outward. Its sides were occupied by the Palazzo dei Portici Settentrionali, with the arch of the **Vittorio Emanuele II Gallery** (Itinerary 7) in the middle, and the Palazzo dei Portici Meridionali. In accordance with the eclectic taste that largely reshaped the face of the historical centre of Milan in the second half of the 19th century, the buildings were based on the model of the Renaissance palazzo. Provision was also made for the construction of a loggia on the southern side to connect the Palazzo dei Portici with the long wing of the Palazzo Reale right in front of the arched entrance to the gallery, where the **Arengario**, which houses the Museum of the 20th Century, now stands (Itinerary 5). Mengoni had also planned a third building, the Palazzo dell'Indipendenza, to stand on the side opposite the Cathedral in the area of the Monument to Vittorio Emanuele II by Ettore Rosa (1896). This would have made the piazza more balanced and compact in scale. The **Duomo** (Cathedral) is the largest and most complex Gothic building in Italy. It is 157 metres in length and its main spire – on which the gilded statue of Our Lady known as the *Madonnina* and regarded as the symbol of

The entrance to the Vittorio Emanuele II Gallery from Piazza del Duomo

Ettore Rosa's Monument to Vittorio Emanuele II, 1896

the city was placed in 1774 – is 108.5 metres in height. The history of its construction and decoration, which began in 1386, continued in various stages until the beginning of the 19th century. Work on its completion has given way in the last two centuries to restoration and conservation, including the crucial step of creating the Museo del Duomo. Among other things, this museum now houses many important and perishable works whose place in the cathedral has been taken by copies.

One of the main advocates of the founding of a new cathedral was Gian Galeazzo Visconti. The problem immediately arose, however, of reaching a compromise with the demands of the local architects and stone carvers who were involved in the great project. As a result, while the choice of marble wall facings reflects models from beyond the Alps, the legacy of Romanesque architecture as developed in the Po Valley can be seen in the sloping aisles and an accentuated width not balanced by corresponding vertical development. Albeit with the significant exceptions of the façade, dome and presbytery, the layout and prospect largely correspond to the ideas crystallised at the end of the 14th century and the decoration also remained faithful to the flowery elegance of International Gothic over the centuries. Visitors are surprised by the wealth of sculptural ornamentation, with over 3,000 statues and hundreds of figures carved in high relief to form an endless parade reaching its peaks in the 14th-century work of Giovannino de' Grassi, the Renaissance classicism of Briosco, Bambaia and Fusina, and the intense activity of the 18th century. The most interesting sections of the exterior are the polygonal apse, which is also the most ancient part, and the sides, with their stupendous blossoming of flying buttresses, windows and statuary. The statues adorning the outsides include 96 gigantic gargoyles constituting an extraordinary and highly imaginative gallery of monstrous and grotesque figures. The façade is the result of two successive stages of construction. The first took place in the 17th century and regarded the lower section, drawing inspiration from the forms of Roman classicism introduced into the Cathedral by Carlo Borromeo's architect Pellegrino Tibaldi. Neo-Gothic in form, the second instead took place at the beginning of the 19th century by order of Napoleon, who had chosen Milan's Cathedral as the setting for his imperial coronation. The design by Leopoldo Pollack involved the transplanting of neoclassical elements extraneous to the general appearance of the building. Carved with flower, fruit and animal motifs, the central portal has a tympanum with a bas-relief depicting the *Creation of Eve* based on drawings by Cerano, an artist of the Counter-Reformation period. The interior is divided into five aisles and characterised by the presence of gigantic Gothic piers with capitals supporting a frieze of statues in niches. The transept is divided into three aisles and the choir is surrounded by an ambulatory and flanked by two rectangular sacristies. The presbytery

Glimpse of the spires of the Cathedral

Following pages
Cathedral, view of the interior

21

was restructured by Tibaldi toward the end of the 16th century. The octagonal dome with ribbed vaulting above the crossing was completed in the 16th century. Its design involved complex problems of static engineering and the efforts of various architects including Filarete, Leonardo da Vinci, Bramante, Francesco di Giorgio Martini and Giovanni Antonio Amadeo. It was actually built by the latter, who also worked for the dukes of Milan in the Carthusian Monastery or Charterhouse of Pavia. Despite all the losses, alterations and additions, the Cathedral still has a remarkable wealth of stained glass windows dating back as far as the early 15th century. The altars crowning the side aisles and the chapels of the transept were mostly designed by Tibaldi and reflect the Counter-Reformation idea of restrained religious feeling subordinate to the authority of the Church. *The Funeral Monument of Gian Giacomo Medici* in the southern arm of the transept is the work of Leone Leoni (1560–1563). A stairway starting in front of the door to the southern sacristy provides access to the *Tesoro del Duomo* (Treasure of the Cathedral), where the priceless collection of treasures includes various outstanding items from the early Middle Ages. The *Trivulzio Candelabra*, which takes its name from the archpriest who donated it to the Cathedral in 1562, can be seen in the northern arm of the transept. Identifiable as largely Gothic in workmanship, possibly of the Rhenish school, this work in bronze is decorated with scenes from the Old Testament divided by tendrils and spiral motifs.

The roof of the Cathedral can be reached by means of a lift installed in one of the buttresses. Among the rich profusion of flying arches, spires, pinnacles and statues visible from here, attention should be drawn in particular to the Carelli spire by the lift, which is the most ancient, the late Gothic spire of Amadeo (1507–1518) on the structure encasing the dome, and the 18th-century main spire crowning the dome itself. Before leaving the church, visitors can descend a narrow staircase set in the inner wall of the façade to see the early Christian archaeological excavations with remains of the **Ambrosian Baptistery of San Giovanni alle Fonti** and the apses of the **Summer Cathedral of Santa Tecla**. No visit to the Cathedral can be regarded as complete if it does not include the **Museo del Duomo** (Museum of the Cathedral), founded in 1953 and located in the Palazzo Reale. The Museum's collection consists primarily of works removed from the Cathedral in order to ensure their preservation, above all sculptures but also windows and paintings. The items are arranged in chronological order from the origins to the 20th century and also include architectural and sculptural models as well as ecclesiastical furnishings and vestments

Walking away from the Cathedral and continuing right through the northern stretch of porticos, we come into **Via dei Mercanti**, which was built in the 19th century in connection with the restructuring of the ancient

The *Quadroni di San Carlo*

Among the cathedral's pictorial riches, particular importance attaches to a series of very large canvases popularly known as the *Quadroni di San Carlo*, which are exhibited in the nave and transept from November to December. These are all that remains of the sumptuous decorations created to celebrate the beatification and canonisation of Carlo Borromeo, bishop of Milan.

The works were commissioned by Carlo's cousin Federico Borromeo during his own reign as bishop and constitute an authentic compendium of early 17th-century Lombard painting, characterised by a marked narrative vein and sincere devotion to the stern and impassioned religious values embodied by the saint.

The leading artists of the period were involved in this undertaking, including above all Giovan Battista Crespi, known as Cerano, and Giulio Cesare Procaccini. In the first case, impetuous and enthralling eloquence is combined with daring compositional and chromatic inventions that show the influence of the painter's studies in Rome as part of Federico's retinue. In the second, warm hues and silken iridescence conjure up a sometimes languid atmosphere of greater intimacy.

Giovan Battista Crespi, known as Cerano, *Saint Carlo Visiting Plague Victims in the Countryside*, from the series of the *Quadroni di San Carlo*, 1602 Cathedral

Cathedral, view of the interior with the *Quadroni di San Carlo* displayed in the nave

Piazza del Broletto Nuovo, a square of arcaded buildings that once housed the chief magistrate (*podestà*) of the city-state, the municipal authorities and the corporations of merchants. The piazza, which dated from the 13th century, was a closed and elevated square with five gateways. The porticos and central area were occupied by commercial enterprises.

Standing on the right side of the street is the **Palazzo dei Giureconsulti**, which still preserves the layout of its 16th-century façade with an elegant loggia of twin columns crowned by a row of windows adorned with reliefs and mouldings despite numerous operations of enlargement, demolition and rebuilding. The rich and eclectic interiors of this multifunctional building currently house the Milan Chamber of Commerce.

The portico of the **Palazzo della Ragione**, which once stood in the middle of the piazza, is located on the left side. Also known as the Palazzo del Broletto Nuovo, it housed the Chamber of the Council of 900 and the Courts, and was built by the *podestà* Oldrado da Tresseno, who is

Palazzo della Ragione, view of the portico

Maestro campionese, *Saint Catherine*, second or third decade of the 14th century Loggia degli Osii

depicted in the relief in the style of Benedetto Antelami on the façade looking onto the Piazza dei Mercanti on the other side of the arcade. The row of triple lancet windows above the round arches of the ground floor corresponds to the great hall, divided in two sections and currently used to stage exhibitions. The top floor was built in the 18th century.

The buildings looking onto **Piazza dei Mercanti**, which include the 14th-century **Loggia degli Osii** on the longer side, show evidence of a series of building operations undertaken in the late 19th and early 20th century to renovate the existing structures or reconstruct the ancient buildings with original elements and masonry, sometimes of heterogeneous origin.

Continuing along Via dei Mercanti, we arrive in **Piazza Cordusio**, which was also part of an immense redevelopment project involving the area between the Piazza del Duomo and the Castle at the turn of the century. The Cordusio – a toponym derived from *curtis ducis* and indicating that this was the location of the ducal court in the Longobard era – stands on an area once occupied by the Roman imperial palace. Adorned in the middle with a Monument to the Poet Giuseppe Parini, it was built as a financial centre lined with imposing edifices such as the Assicurazioni Generali Building designed by Luca Beltrami, the old Stock Exchange Building (now occupied by the Post Office) and the headquarters of the Credito Italiano Bank. From the Cordusio we proceed along **Via Dante**, another fulcrum of the 'Umbertine' urban-planning scheme (developed in the reign of Umberto I, 1878–1900). The street runs perpendicular to the Castle, which acts as a backdrop, and cuts diagonally through the grid of the old city. As a result, the buildings on the corners take on a distinctive appearance. Those lining the street were built in the closing decades of the 19th century for housing and shops. In accordance with the special regulations issued, all the buildings were to be of the same height and a competition was held for the best architectural work. The winner was the **Palazzo Richard-Ginori**, designed by Giuseppe Pirovano, at number 13. Before reaching this, we pass the intersection with Via del Rovello on the right, where the building at number 2 is the sole survivor of the Umbertine Urban Clearance Project. This is the **Palazzo del Carmagnola**, a gift to the renowned soldier of fortune of that name from Filippo Maria Visconti and later owned by Cecilia Gallerani, the favourite of Ludovico Sforza, known as Ludovico il Moro (the Moor). Next to the palace stands the **Paolo Grassi Theatre**, the former headquarters of the **Piccolo Teatro**, one of the best-known theatrical establishments in Milan, set up by Paolo Grassi and Giorgio Strehler.

An imposing **Monument to Garibaldi** (1895) by Ettore Ximenes stands in the middle of Largo Cairoli at the end of Via Dante. On the other side of this square, the two concentric semi-circles of Piazza Castello and the **Foro Buonaparte** occupied a vast area near the Castle previously used for military purposes. While the plans drawn up for this area, known as the Foro Buonaparte, by Giovanni Antonio Antolini in 1801 were never put into effect, they provided at least a basis for the projects carried out at the end of the century. Flanked by elegant residential works of historicist architecture, the two curving stretches of the Foro Buonaparte made it possible to connect the block of Piazza Cordusio and Via Dante, and therefore the historical

centre, with the new districts constructed to the west of the Castle. Running left out of Largo Cairoli, Via San Giovanni sul Muro follows the line of the Roman city walls. Standing at the beginning of the street is the **Church of Santa Maria della Consolazione**, built by Galeazzo Maria Sforza in 1471 but renovated in the 19th century, where we can see some paintings by Camillo Procaccini. If we instead proceed along the right-hand stretch of the Foro Buonaparte, by the corner with Via Tivoli we find two theatres, the **Giorgio Strehler** and the **Studio Melato**, named after the actress Mariangela Melato, who passed away in 2013. As the new home of the Piccolo Teatro, they constitute the sort of theatre precinct dreamt of by the two founders Paolo Grassi and Giorgio Strehler. The main building, designed by Marco Zanuso, displays postmodern leanings and is an important point of reference at the urban level.

The final goal of this itinerary is the **Castello Sforzesco** (Sforza Castle) with its museums and natural connection with the Sempione Park. Its history began in 1358, when Galeazzo II of the Visconti family had a fortress built in the western part of the city near the gate known as Porta Giovia. In later generations, the Castle became the residence of the rulers of Milan, who had previously lived in a palace alongside the Cathedral. Its period of greatest splendour came with the reigns of Francesco, Galeazzo Maria and then Ludovico Sforza. First, it was entirely rebuilt

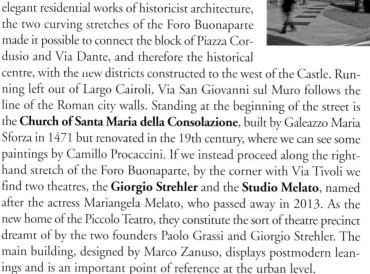

Piazza Cordusio

Sforza Castle, view of Ettore Ximenes' Monument to Garibaldi, 1895

Sforza Castle,
the façade with
the Filarete Tower

Following pages
Sforza Castle,
Piazza d'Armi

in the form of a square fortress with a tower at each of its four corners. One of the architects was the Tuscan Filarete, whose work included re-designing the façade looking onto the city and a monumental entrance tower that collapsed during a battle in 1521. The subsequent work of decoration involved artists such as Vincenzo Foppa and Leonardo da Vinci. Summoned to Milan by Ludovico il Moro, Leonardo frescoed several rooms together with other artists and produced a celebrated design for an Equestrian Monument to Francesco Sforza, which was to have stood in front of the main façade.

Having lost all of its residential functions, the Castle became a solid and well-fortified stronghold in the 17th and 18th centuries complete with a moat and a complex star-shaped system of bastions stretching for over three kilometres. Napoleon had these walls demolished in 1796, thus creating a vast empty space around the building and paving the way for a change in its use. It was, however, not until 1893, when it became the property of the city of Milan, that the Castle embarked on the new phase stretching up to the present, subjected to radical restoration by the architect Luca Beltrami and converted to house cultural institutions of great prestige. A shrine of memories, symbol of rediscovered ideals of freedom, fulcrum of the city's social and political history and key monument of the city's late 19th-century planning scheme, it was restored to the ideal splendour it enjoyed under the Sforza dynasty. Scholarly research on architectural remains and documents made it possible to restore an ideal stylistic unity oblivious to the stratification of time through a complex campaign of demolition and reconstruction. The battlements of the walls and towers were rebuilt together with the ogival windows and their terracotta frames. The outer walls were decorated with plaster and sgraffito work. The ducal apartments were restructured and restored together with their fresco decorations. The Main Tower (or Filarete Tower) was completely rebuilt, renamed for Umberto I and inaugurated in 1904.

The Castle presents four uniform façades to the outside world, the one in front being dominated by the **Filarete Tower** and flanked by two cylindrical towers as opposed to the square towers at the rear. Gates are cut into the façades. The loggia on the right side known as the Ponticella di Ludovico il Moro is attributed to Bramante but was largely rebuilt in the 19th century. The remains of a ravelin that connected the building with the ring of fortifications can be seen on the left side.

The Castle is organised internally around three courtyards. The first, which can be reached from the main tower, is the **Parade Ground**, a simple enclosed space with modern buildings on two sides. Together with similar elements to be found in various parts of the complex, the archaeological materials and remains of ancient Milanese buildings laid out in the area on the right bear witness to plans to make the residence of the Sforza fam-

1

ily a Museum of the City. Known as the **Cortile della Rocchetta**, the courtyard opening to the left on the other side of the parade ground lies before a group of buildings laid out as a citadel, to which the family would withdraw in moments of greatest danger. Visitors entering from the parade ground have an arcade structure attributed to Filarete on their left and one attributed to Bramante in front of them. A fresco depicting *Argus* and attributed to Donato Bramante and Bramantino can be seen in the **Sala del Tesoro** (the Treasury Room) on the ground floor of the corner tower. Opening off the Cortile della Rocchetta to the right is the **Cortile della Corte Ducale**, a courtyard surrounded on three sides by a building that contained the ducal halls of state. The Renaissance arcade on the far side is known as the Elephant Portico. The two-storey loggia closing the left side provides access to a Renaissance staircase largely rebuilt by Beltrami and the entrance to the collections is on the right side of the courtyard. The ducal apartments can be visited as part of the Collection of Sculpture. Laid out in the setting designed by the BBPR group, champions of modern architecture in Milan after World War II, the **Collection of Sculpture** covers a span of time from late antiquity to the Middle Ages and the Renaissance. Most of the sculptures are from ancient Milanese and Lombard buildings that no longer exist. Attention should be drawn in particular to the section devoted to the corporation of craftsmen known as the *maestri campionesi*, including the Funeral Monuments

Cortile della Rocchetta

Bramantino (Bartolomeo Suardi), *Argus*, 1489–1491 Sforza Castle, Cortile della Rocchetta, Trivulziana Library, Treasury Room

36

37

Michelangelo's *Rondanini Pietà*

Purchased by the Municipal Museums of Milan in 1952, this is traditionally held to be Michelangelo's last work. The master was still working on the sculpture as his life drew to a close and it was in his home at the moment of his death on 18 February 1564. It is commonly known as the *Rondanini Pietà* from the name of the aristocratic Roman family that bought it in the 18th century. The grief of Mary over the body of Jesus is a recurrent theme in the artist's late work, and the marked difference between the mature interpretations and the early work in Saint Peter's in Rome clearly highlights Michelangelo's development not only in stylistic but also in intensely personal and spiritual terms. Michelangelo worked on a block of marble already used a few years earlier to sketch out another version of the same subject, which he had evidently found unsatisfactory. As Vasari observed, his judgement was so fine that he was never content with what he did. Eliminating the earlier head and chest of Christ (but leaving the legs and a redundant arm), he fashioned both figures out of the part of the block originally intended for Mary alone. The resulting sense of extreme simplification, indissoluble unity and upward impetus characterising this composition is all the more astonishing in view of its absolute modernity by comparison with the winding lines and spiral construction of contemporary late Mannerist work. Sacrificing anatomical perfection, volumetric definition and the moulding of surfaces, Michelangelo obtained the effect of heightened spirituality and transcendence of matter that is the hallmark of his 'unfinished' figures. The idea is that the figure somehow living and imprisoned within the stone be set free from the material by the sculptor with his chisel. The marks left on the marble, now restored to its ancient lustre through recent cleaning, reveal the vigour with which the artist 'attacked' the block to be sculpted. The recently inaugurated **Museo Pietà Rondanini_Michelangelo** houses the sculptural masterpiece in the former Ospedale Spagnolo (Spanish Hospital) inside Sforza Castle, which has been especially restored for the occasion.

Michelangelo Buonarroti, *Rondanini Pietà*, 1564

of Bernabò Visconti and his wife Regina della Scala from the Church of San Giovanni in Conca. The Equestrian Statue of Bernabò by Bonino da Camione is flanked by figures symbolising strength and wisdom.

Known as the **Sala delle Asse**, room 8 was the most important chamber of the Sforza court. It was the reception hall of Ludovico il Moro, according to tradition, and still bears the remains of pictorial decoration which can be attributed on the basis of documentary evidence to Leonardo da Vinci. Rediscovered during the restoration of the Castle and largely retouched, the paintings show a sort of pavilion made out of the interwoven branches of sixteen trees and a rope of gold knotted at intervals. There are also traces of a rocky landscape on the walls. The portraits of the Sforza family in the small adjoining room (*Saletta Negra*) are attributed to Bernardino Luini and come from a building on Corso Magenta. Further on we come to the Ducal Chapel with its 15th-century frescoes.

The Sections of Gothic Sculpture and Lombard Renaissance Sculpture are also richly endowed, the latter including works by Giovanni Antonio Amadeo and Cristoforo Mantegazza, a series of portals (including the celebrated Entrance to the Medici Bank by Tuscan artists) and numerous pieces of the Monumental Tomb of Gaston de Foix, the military commander of Francis I of France. This huge work by Bambaia was left un-

Sforza Castle, detail of the ceiling of the Sala delle Asse decorated by Leonardo da Vinci, circa 1498

Lombard craftsman,
Coretto di Torchiara,
1450–1475
Sforza Castle,
Antique Furnishings
Collection, room 17

finished on the collapse of French domination in 1522 and its scattered component parts ended up in different collections. Most of them have now been gathered together in the Castle, including the recumbent statue of the deceased and a series of bas-reliefs celebrating his deeds.

The series of rooms also exhibit a rich array of armour, swords and firearms. Visitors can proceed directly from the Collection of Sculpture to the first floor, which houses the Pinacoteca (Picture Gallery) and the **Antique Furnishings Collection** of the **Museum of Decorative Arts**. Rearranged in 2004 for exhibition in four rooms, this consists primarily of domestic furniture made in Lombardy and northern Italy together with tapestries, paintings, jewellery and ceramics. In addition to the substantial group of Renaissance chests, attention should be drawn to the works from the Castle of Torrechiara in the province of Parma. These include the *Coretto*, a private box of finely inlaid wood making it possible to attend religious functions without being seen, and a series of 24 grisaille frescoes telling the story of Griselda from the Boccaccio's *Decameron*. One room is devoted to the ancient *Wunderkammern* or cabinets of curiosities, collections of extraordinary objects of various nature and origin ranging from natural history to precious and sophisticated artefacts. In addition to a number of nautilus shells fashioned into ornate drinking vessels, the items include the Cabinet of the Canon Passalacqua (a miniature building with niches, statues and paintings) and the Settala Automaton, an ancient mechanical figure capable of moving and producing diabolical noises. The Collection also holds some significant 18th-century items from the workshop of Giuseppe Maggiolini, which was celebrated for complex and elegant inlaid decorations, and a range of 20th-century furniture by designers such as Gio Ponti and Ettore Sottsass.

Arranged to include also medals, bas-reliefs and sculptures, the **Pinacoteca** (Picture Gallery) hosts paintings from historical buildings that are now municipal property, frescoes from churches and mansions in Lombardy, and works formerly belonging to munificent Milanese collectors. The result is a varied and heterogeneous collection that is in any case primarily

Andrea Mantegna,
*The Trivulzio
Madonna*, 1497

laid out so as to focus on Lombard painting over the period from the 15th century to the 18th. The theme of the private collection is addressed in particular in room 23, which celebrates the purchase by public subscription of the Trivulzio Collection with masterpieces by painters such as Andrea Mantegna, Antonello da Messina, Filippo Lippi and Giovanni Bellini. One recent acquisition is a splendid Madonna and Child (circa 1495) – known as the *Lia Madonna* from the name of the collector who generously donated it to the city – by Francesco Napoletano, a pupil of Leonardo da Vinci. Among the Lombard artists of the Renaissance era, particular importance attaches to Vincenzo Foppa, the founder of the Lombard school and a painter with an exquisite handling of chiaroscuro and capacity for truth and substance. Room 25 compares Venetian painting as exemplified by masters such as Titian and Tintoretto with the schools of Bergamo and Brescia, which came under its influ-

Canaletto (Giovanni Antonio Canal), *The Pier near Riva degli Schiavoni with the Column of the Lion of Saint Mark*, before 1742

Canaletto (Giovanni Antonio Canal), *The Pier near Riva degli Schiavoni with the Column of Saint Theodore*, before 1742

1

ence. A very large section (room 26) is devoted to painters of the Counter-Reformation period such as Morazzone, Cerano, Daniele Crespi and Giulio Cesare Procaccini, who made Milan one of the capitals of early Italian Baroque. The series of rooms ends with 18th-century portraitists like Fra' Galgario and Giacomo Ceruti, whose works combine descriptive and material precision with a very modern capacity for psychological and social investigation, and 18th-century views of Venice with paintings by Canaletto, Francesco Guardi and Bernardo Bellotto.

Other sections of the Museum of Decorative Arts are located in the old citadel or *Rocchetta*, which can be reached from the general museum entrance, together with the **Museum of Musical Instruments**. Supranational in its breadth, this collection consists of hundreds of items documenting the evolution of the different types of instrument (wind, string and keyboard). Particular attention is focused on the crafting of stringed

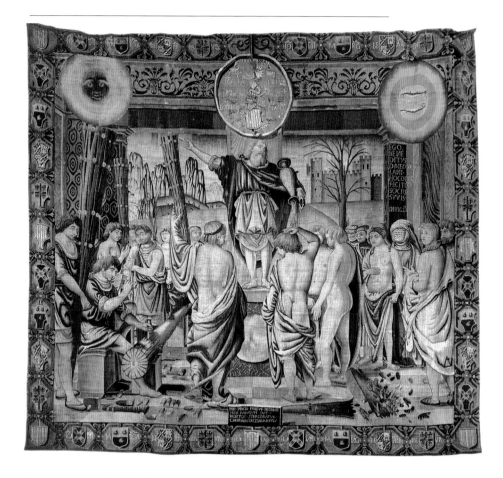

instruments, which had its key centres in the region of Lombardy in Brescia, Cremona and Milan itself. A small section is devoted to Non-European Instruments.

Taking its name from a game played in the days of the Sforza dynasty, the **Sala della Balla** is the room exhibiting the extraordinary series of *Trivulzio Tapestries* produced around 1503 by the ducal factories at Vigevano. The compositions are based on designs by the Milanese painter Bramantino and allegorically present the months of the year in monumental forms and splendid colours.

The upper floor of the Rocchetta houses the **Collection of Applied Arts** including glassware, ceramics, jewellery, fans, bronzes and technical and scientific instruments. The sections of particular interest include the large selection of Murano glassware, the Italian Renaissance majolica, and the Lombard ceramics stretching from the 17th and 18th centuries up to some significant items produced in the first half of the 20th. The Collection

Benedetto da Milano (cartoon by Bartolomeo Suardi, known as Bramantino), tapestry depicting the month of *February*, from the series of *Trivulzio Tapestries*, circa 1503 Sforza Castle, Museum of Decorative Arts, Sala della Balla

Municipal
Aquarium, view
of the façade
with the statue
of *Neptune*

1

of Ivory is international in character and covers a span of time from late antiquity to the 18th century with statuettes, diptychs, tabernacles and caskets. The gallery in room 30 displays items from the Fashion and Clothing Collection and Non-European Collections on a rotating basis.

The basements of the Rocchetta, the entrance to which is in the courtyard, house the **Prehistoric and Proto-Historic** and **Egyptian Sections** of the Municipal Archaeological and Numismatic Collections (Itinerary 4). Importance attaches in the Prehistoric and Proto-Historic Section to the artefacts of the Golasecca culture and the Egyptian Section presents an interesting group of painted sarcophaguses.

From the courtyard of the ducal court, the Barchio Gate led in Renaissance times to the garden, which was then occupied by the Spanish fortifications. After the demolition ordered by Napoleon, the area was used as a military parade ground and became a focal point for various speculative building projects. Finally, plans drawn up by Emilio Alemagna established the boundaries of the present-day **Parco Sempione** (Sempione Park), the city's largest park, in 1893. Laid out in the English style with picturesque paths winding around a small lake and a wealth of exotic trees and rare plants, the park also includes a number of buildings and some modern monuments.

Milan hosted the International Exhibition organised in 1906 to celebrate the completion of the Sempione Tunnel and some of the 225 structures erected for the occasion were located in the park. The sole survivor is the building on the right side of the park that now houses the **Acquario Civico** (Municipal Aquarium) in Viale Gadio 2. Rebuilt in its original form after the bombing of World War II and recently modernised, the building has a façade in the Viennese Secession style and decorative elements in majolica and relief of an aquatic nature arranged around a Fountain of Neptune. The **Arena**, an oval-shaped amphitheatre dating from the Napoleonic era and presenting four neoclassical façades with columns, tympanums and arches, is located a short distance away. Among other things, it could originally be filled with water from the Naviglio Canal and used to stage sea battles.

Among the monuments to be seen in the greenery as we proceed toward the heart of the park, attention should be drawn to *Accumulazione Musicale e Seduta* by Arman and *Bagni Misteriosi*, a painted and sculptural fountain by Giorgio de Chirico. These two works were created in 1973 on the occasion of the 15th Milan Triennial, which set itself the objective of placing special artistic structures for rest and recreation in the setting of the city's parks. From here one can see the back façade of the **Palazzo dell'Arte**, home to the **Triennale di Milano**.

The works to be seen as we continue toward the end of the park include a **Library** by Ico Parisi and Silvio Longhi (1954) and the **Torre Branca**, a tower of steel pipes designed by a team including Gio Ponti and built in 1932 in accordance with Mussolini's wishes. The **Arco della Pace** (Arch of Peace) aligned with the Sforza Castle at the exit from the park marks the beginning of Corso Sempione, the first stretch of the Napoleonic highway to France. It is now lined with 20th-century buildings, some of which are quite noteworthy. Designed by Luigi Cagnola and begun in 1807, the arch was completed in 1838 during the period of Austrian rule. Originally conceived to celebrate Napoleon's victories, it was instead dedicated to the peace treaty of 1815 and the Restoration, as can be seen from the events depicted in the bas-reliefs. The bronze group of the six-horse Chariot of Peace (*La Sestiga della Pace*) on the top of the monument is accompanied by a Statue of Victory at each of the four corners. The **Certosa** (Carthusian Monastery or Charterhouse) **of Garegnano** can be reached by proceeding all the way down Corso Sempione and then continuing along a stretch of Viale Certosa. (The distance is about

Triennale di Milano, Triennale Design Museum

The **Triennale di Milano**, established in Monza in 1923 as the first Biennial of Decorative Arts, has been located since 1933 in Milan in the Palazzo dell'Arte, designed by Giovanni Muzio and built between autumn 1931 and spring 1933. Conceived by Muzio as an extremely flexible container, it represents an innovative multiuse organism for the period in which it was designed. The Triennale di Milano has become a reference point in the city's cultural and economic life, the driving force of an intense dialogue between society and the world of creativity. Each day it hosts exhibitions on architecture, design, art, communications and fashion; it organises conferences and debates; it offers places of study and research, such as the Biblioteca del Progetto (Project Library), along with

services to the public, like the Bookstore, the Triennale Design Café and the open-air DesignCafé nestled in the lush Parco Sempione.

In December 2007 the **Triennale Design Museum** was inaugurated; it represents the multiplicity of expressions of Italian design. It is a dynamic museum able to offer visitors unique and diversified outlooks, points of view and itineraries, renewing itself continuously through a system of representations that each year changes themes, scientific orderings and exhibition designs. The museum manages a vast network of 'layerings' present throughout Italy (private collections, company museums, specialised collections and small themed museums) with which it has established a close collaborative relationship. The studio of Achille Castiglioni is one of these design 'layerings'. The Triennale di Milano has kept it alive, working to preserve and enhance its material.

Triennale Design Museum, entrance

Triennale di Milano, façade

five kilometres or three miles and it is better to take the train from the Cadorna station to Certosa, which takes just a few minutes.) Founded by Giovanni Visconti in 1349, it originally stood in a forest infested by brigands. Petrarch visited it frequently during his stay in Milan, and described it as 'beautiful and noble'. Its present appearance, characterised by a tall and richly decorated façade divided horizontally into three sections, is the result of a 16th-century project of expansion and restructuring, possibly the work of Pellegrino Tibaldi. It has been described as the 'Sistine Chapel of Milan' on the strength of the series of frescoes painted by Daniele Crespi on the ceiling and walls of the nave in 1629. Harmonising fully with the atmosphere of simple devotion and contemplation proper to such a place and above all with the lifestyle of the Carthusian monks, the paintings illustrate episodes from the life of Saint Brunone. The dominant greys and purples and the numerous figures of monks with different expressions and attitudes constitute the salient characteristics. Paintings by other artists ranging from the late 16th to the 18th century can be seen in the presbytery and chapels of the church as well as the chapter room and refectory of the monastery.

Daniele Crespi, *Histories from the Life of Saint Brunone*, detail, 1629

Certosa of Garegnano, view of the apse with Simone Peterzano's *Crucifixion*

From Piazza del Duomo to Corso Magenta:
Through the History of the City
from Its Origins to the 20th Century

2

The itinerary runs through the western districts of the city and takes in some monumental complexes emblematically representing phases of crucial importance in its history: from Roman times (the layout of the area around the Stock Exchange and the Archaeological Museum), the medieval era (the Basilica of Sant'Ambrogio), the Sforza dynasty (the Churches of San Maurizio and Santa Maria delle Grazie) and the Borromeo family (Piazza Borromeo and the Ambrosian Library) all the way to more recent history with the industrial development documented by the Science and Technology Museum and the new Art Nouveau buildings as well as the latest work by contemporary architects in the Bovisa district and Piazzale Lotto.

From Piazza del Duomo we take Via degli Orefici, part of a system of blocks including Via Armorari and Via Spadari that was demolished and rebuilt at the beginning of the 20th century, and then turn left into Via Cesare Cantù. This leads us into Piazza Pio XI in front of the building that houses the **Biblioteca** and **Pinacoteca Ambrosiana** (Ambrosian Library and Picture Gallery) founded at the beginning of the 17th century by Cardinal Federico Borromeo.

As it now stands, the building is the result of three phases of construction, the first (1603–1605) involving the building of the library; its façade with the original entrance is still visible in Piazza San Sepolcro. This was a building of small size and elongated shape occupied by a succession of rooms and dominated by the **Sala Federiciana**, a barrel-vaulted reading room flooded with light from its large semicircular windows. The founding of the Pinacoteca (1618) then necessitated the building of a new annex, which was completed in 1630. Further additions were made in the neoclassical era, including the façade on Piazza Pio XI (the present entrance) and a large courtyard subsequently converted into a new reading room. The building underwent restructuring and restoration in the

Biblioteca
Ambrosiana, Sala
Federiciana

53

20th century, some of which was connected with the bombing in 1943. The last project to reorganise the exhibition area was completed in 1997. The holdings of the Library, the first in Europe to be opened to the public, includes a vast collection of codices and manuscripts, with particular importance attaching to the celebrated *Virgilio* annotated by Petrarch and illuminated by Simone Martini. Attention should be drawn among the numerous autograph works to Piero della Francesca's *De perspectiva pingendi* and the celebrated *Codex Atlanticus* of Leonardo da Vinci, purchased in 1637 and now viewable by the public in the Ambrosiana itself and in the Sala del Bramante in Santa Maria delle Grazie.

At its foundation, the Pinacoteca had approximately 250 original paintings and copies. Today, as a result of numerous donations, the collection comprises over 1,500 works. These are divided into schools for display purposes in accordance with the original intentions of the cardinal, who had conceived the Gallery as a complement to the courses of the Accademia del Disegno, the Art Academy founded in 1620 and relocated to the Palazzo di Brera in 1775 (Itinerary 7). The works of greatest interest include the *Ritratto di musico* (Portrait of a Musician) by Leonardo da Vinci and the *Canestro di frutta* (Still Life with Basket of

Caravaggio (Michelangelo Merisi), *Still Life with Basket of Fruit*, 1594–1598 Pinacoteca Ambrosiana

Leonardo da Vinci, *Portrait of a Musician*, circa 1485 Pinacoteca Ambrosiana

55

Fruit) by Caravaggio, the latter of which belonged to Federico. It was also the cardinal that purchased Raphael's huge preparatory drawing (800 × 285 cm) for his celebrated fresco *La Scuola di Atene* (The School of Athens) in the Vatican. The founder's interests also included the Leonardesque painters, especially Bernardino Luini, and Titian as well as genre painting as exemplified by the landscapes and still-life works of leading Flemish artists of the period, such as Paul Brill and Jan Breughel the Elder, also known as Velvet Breughel. Together with his paintings, the cardinal also donated a very important collection of drawings and prints and a collection of sculptures. Among the acquisitions subsequent to these donations, attention should be drawn to the 17th-century Scientific Museum of Manfredo Settala, a collection comprising a large library, stuffed exotic animals, skeletons of birds and fish, various scientific instruments and a mechanical automaton. Part of the collection has been transferred to other Milanese cultural institutions, including the Museum of Decorative Arts in the Sforza Castle (Itinerary 1) and the Municipal Museum of Natural History (Itinerary 6).

The two streets running alongside the Biblioteca Ambrosiana lead into **Piazza San Sepolcro**, which is built on an area once occupied by a Roman forum. The layout of this part of the city still partly reflects the grid of the settlement in the 1st century BC. It was here, in the assembly hall of the Alleanza Industriale, that the Fascist movement was founded on 23 March 1919 at a gathering with approximately three hundred participants led by Benito Mussolini. This is why the original form of Fascism is also referred to as *Sansepolcrismo*. The buildings looking onto the piazza include the side of the Ambrosian Library with its original entrance and the **Church of San Sepolcro**, founded in 1030 and given its present dedication to the Holy Sepulchre at the time of the second crusade, led by the Milanese archbishop Anselmo IV. While the present Romanesque façade was built at the end of the 19th century, the interior retains the form it took in the 17th century after restoration by Federico Borromeo. Particular interest attaches to some sculptural groups, including ten terracotta statues of the 16th-century Lombard school forming a *Deposition* (the *Christ* is not original) in the crypt, whose almost intact structure is the only surviving part of the medieval church built as a copy of the Church of the Holy Sepulchre in Jerusalem. The groups at the sides of the presbytery representing two mysteries of the Passion form part of a project initiated by Carlo Borromeo but later abandoned. Tradition has it that the great sarcophagus in the centre of the nave once contained earth brought back from Jerusalem by crusaders and a lock of the Virgin Mary's hair. Crafted by a member of the corporation of *maestri campionesi* (craftsmen coming from the Como-Ticino area) in the early 14th century, it is decorated with a relief depicting Christ's burial.

Having proceeded along Via del Bollo as far as the crossroads known as the Cinque Vie, we can turn left toward Palazzo Borromeo and the Church of Santa Maria Podone or right toward the Piazza degli Affari. The **Church of Santa Maria Podone** looks onto the square, which is still the property of the Borromeo family. Founded in the 11th century, the church came under the protection of this ancient branch of the Milanese aristocracy in the 15th century. Its present appearance, with a façade modelled on an arch of triumph and an interior with three aisles, is largely the result of rebuilding carried out in the 17th century by the cardinal Federico. The polygonal shape of the late Gothic Chapel of the Borromeo family (15th century) can be seen on the right side. All that remains of the fresco decoration that Federico commissioned Bartolomeo Genovesino to paint inside is a depiction of *Our Lady of the Assumption* in the apse. The altar and the Gothic-style decoration of the Borromeo Chapel date from the 19th century. Opposite the church is the **Palazzo Borromeo**, a remarkable example of the stately mansions of the 15th century but unfortunately seriously damaged during the bombing of 1943. The façade of exposed terracotta retains its fine doorway with a carved frame of red and pink marble and traces of the ancient ogival windows interspersed with their 17th-century successors. Some of the original octagonal pillars and traces of the ancient façade can still be seen in the two courtyards. Frescoes in the late Gothic style reminiscent of Pisanello's work depicting scenes of courtly life with games and dances can be seen by request in one of the rooms of this private building.

Via Bocchetto leads from the crossroads to **Piazza Edison**, one of the nerve centres of the business district that developed as from the end of the 19th century on the ruins of the ancient buildings in the Cordusio area (Itinerary 1), including churches and monasteries. The imposing **Palazzo della Banca d'Italia** (Bank of Italy Building, 1907–1912), designed by Luigi Broggi, looks onto the square. The architectural vocabulary adopted for the exteriors combines citations of Roman Baroque with cautious borrowings from the Viennese Secession to give the whole a rhetorical and academic character. Turning right off Via delle Poste, we arrive in **Piazza degli Affari**, built as part of a project (1928–1940) to expand the business district. The original plan was for a larger piazza to accommodate all of the city's markets. The northern side is dominated by Paolo Mezzanotte's enormous **Palazzo della Borsa** (Stock Exchange Building, 1931) and its huge façade of travertine decorated with allegorical reliefs and groups. In addition to the Italian stock exchange, it houses the Congress and Training Centre, an ultra-modern centre of multimedia communications. Having lost its role as the heart of the old stock exchange with the advent of computerisation, the trading floor was converted into an auditorium with a futuristic ceiling of crystal and steel set at a new height so as to leave visible the three tiers of balconies and the huge glass roof of Mezzanotte's building. Remains of the walls of a Roman Theatre (1st century AD) can be seen beneath a glass floor in the first basement, previously occupied by the grain market. A series of pillars and their ceramic tiles with female figures and trees of abundance, specially designed by Gio Ponti and produced by Richard-Ginori, are what remains of the facing that covered all the walls of this room, which was designed by Mezzanotte in the shape of an amphitheatre and once housed a restaurant open to the public. Since 2010, the centre of the square opposite the Stock Exchange has been dominated by Maurizio Cattelan's Carrara marble sculpture, provocatively entitled *L.O.V.E. Libertà. Odio. Vendetta. Eternità* (Liberty. Hatred. Vendetta. Eternity). Over four metres tall, it represents a huge hand with severed fingers, except for the mid-

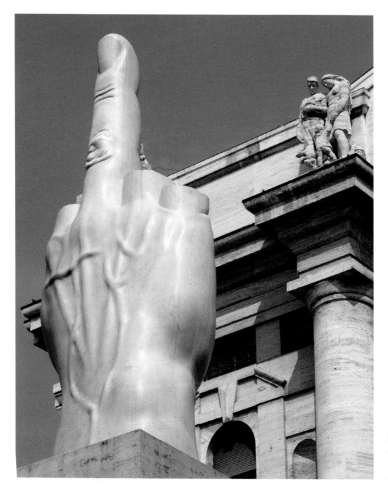

Maurizio Cattelan,
*L.O.V.E. Libertà.
Odio. Vendetta.
Eternità,* 2010

Bernardino Luini, *Ippolita Bentivoglio with Saint Agnes, Saint Scholastica and Saint Catherine*, detail with *Ippolita Bentivoglio* Church of San Maurizio al Monastero Maggiore

dle finger, to reproduce an irreverent, provocative gesture. It was initially installed as a temporary work, until it finally became municipal property.

Via Santa Maria Fulcorina and Via Santa Maria alla Porta, where we can see the fine 17th-century church of the same name with original furnishings and paintings, lead from Piazza degli Affari to the beginning of Corso Magenta, the thoroughfare that once ran from the Cordusio through the district known as the Borgo delle Grazie to the Spanish walls and the Porta Vercellina (now Porta Magenta).

2

Located immediately on the left is the **Church of San Maurizio al Monastero Maggiore**, formerly part of a convent of Benedictine nuns set to the right of the façade in the place where Via Luini was built in the 19th century (seriously impairing the stability of the ecclesiastical building). Building began in 1503 on the site of an older church and the elegant façade divided by pilasters was completed toward the end of the century with the addition of the upper pediment. The interior is practically intact and presents one of the most complete and interesting cycles of 16th-century Lombard frescoes. The edifice presents the typical partitioned structure of the convent church, with a section accessible from the street open to the public and a wall reaching up to the ceiling just behind the altar to separate this from the area for the convent and the nuns. There is a row of ten chapels on either side of the church below a loggia of Palladian arches with round windows in the wall above. The chapels in the outer section of the church house the tombs of important Milanese families, the two flanking the altar belonging in particular to the Bentivoglio. This family of Bolognese origin was connected with the house of Sforza by marriage to constitute a sort of clan distinguished by its sophisticated culture and courtly way of life. The Monastery of San Maurizio was closely connected with these families in the 16th century, as attested by the fresco portraits of donors on the dividing wall, including Alessandro Bentivoglio and his wife Ippolita Sforza. The figure in a nun's habit identifiable by the attribute of the dove as Saint Scholastica is portrayed with the features of Alessandra Bentivoglio, abbess of the convent. Constituting an extraordinary whole by virtue of its richness and close connection with the architectural structure, the pictorial decoration began when the building work was completed around 1515 and involved several generations of artists. Particular importance attaches to Bernardino Luini, whose works include the frescoes on the dividing wall, splendid examples of his gentle and classically restrained style. *The Adoration of the Magi* in the middle of the wall is a later addition by Antonio Campi. Luini was followed by his sons as well as Callisto Piazza from Lodi and the Venetian Simone Peterzano, who worked there at the end of the 16th century. The part of the church reserved for the nuns, which was probably built first, has an arcade with round paintings or tondos depicting *saints* and *martyrs*. These should be regarded as belonging to an early phase of decoration prior to Luini and involving an unidentified artist's studio, possibly with the participation of the Leonardesque painter Giovanni Antonio Boltraffio. The finely carved wooden choir stalls and the organ, which is still in perfect working order, constituted the original furnishings of this area.

The surviving elements of the ancient Monastery of San Maurizio, namely the entrance and cloister, are incorporated into the building of the **Archaeological Museum** located just after Via Luini. The site is of particular interest due to the presence of valuable remains of the Roman city in the shape of a stretch of the foundations of the walls from the reign of Maximinian, which are visible inside the museum, and what is known as the Tower of Ansperto, archbishop of Milan. Situated in the courtyard, this formed part of the ring of fortifications. The museum is designed for educational purposes, as shown first and foremost by the model reconstruction of Roman Milan in the vestibule. Various sections of the Municipal Archaeological Collections are exhibited in the rooms, others now being housed in the Sforza Castle (Itinerary 1). Among other things, the Etruscan Section presents some precious grave goods and the Greek Section a huge collection of pottery from various cultures of the Mediterranean area, including some jars of remarkable size. The Roman Section is the most extensive, comprising glassware, busts, floors, grave goods and jewellery. The items of greatest importance include the *Trivulzio Cup*, a very rare example of a blown glass goblet set inside an openwork glass cage, and the *Patera of Parabiago*, a large plate of chased and gilded silver depicting the nuptial procession of Cybele and Attis (4th century AD). The Museum also has a Barbarian Section and one devoted to the art of Gandhara, with numerous representations of the Buddha and Siddhartha dating from the 2nd, 3rd and 4th centuries AD.

Standing on the opposite side of the street, **Palazzo Litta** is regarded as one of the more significant works of late Baroque Lombard architecture. Work began on its construction in 1645 to designs by Francesco Maria Ricchino and it was then enlarged in the 18th century. In addi-

Bernardino Luini, *Christ Bound to the Column* Church of San Maurizio al Monastero Maggiore

tion to the dynamic and contrasting façade, the points of interest include the main courtyard, monumental staircase and ballroom (the *Salone degli Specchi* or Hall of Mirrors), where lavish social gatherings were held in the 18th and 19th centuries. Among other things, the palace houses the oldest of Milan's working theatres, originally used for purposes of family entertainment.

Continuing along Corso Magenta, we can turn left into Via Terraggio, which follows the line of the medieval walls, to reach the Basilica of Sant'Ambrogio. On the left before the entrance is a **Temple of Victory** dedicated to those fallen in war and designed by Giovanni Muzio with assistance from a team including Gio Ponti (1927–1930). Taking as its models the Mausoleum of Theoderic in Ravenna and the lines of 16th-century architecture, the monument is crowned with an electrical beacon. The Statue of *Saint Ambrose* in the niche in front to the entrance is the work of Adolfo Wildt. The **Pusterla di Sant'Ambrogio** facing onto the square in front of the basilica was built in 1939 on the model of a postern gate in the medieval walls. Ancient materials are incorporated into the brick towers.

Founded in the 4th century by the bishop Ambrose and subsequently dedicated to him, the **Basilica of Sant'Ambrogio** originally stood outside the Roman walls on the burial place of the saints Gervase and Protase, and was initially known as the *basilica martyrum* for this reason. The renovation work begun in the area of the apse during the 9th century and continued all the way through the 12th gave the building the characteristic appearance of a Romanesque basilica, albeit with some distinctive features. It was in the 11th century that chapels began to be added at the sides. Further construction took place in the 16th century with the rectory, built by Bramante for Ludovico il Moro, and the monastery, which now houses the Catholic University. Carlo Borromeo had the dome rebuilt and Federico ensured that the work involved did not impair the stylistic unity of the building. Plans were drawn up in 1859 to restore the basilica to its hypothetical form in the 12th century, when Romanesque architecture was at its height. All of the vaulted ceilings were demolished and rebuilt, and new pictorial decoration of a neo-medieval character was completed in 1897. Further work became necessary after the bombing in World War II.

The basilica is entered through a columned atrium that presents the external appearance of an austere structure with a series of blind arches. Its interior is instead animated by the alternation of differently coloured materials and the presence of capitals with relief decoration, some salvaged from Roman buildings, some Romanesque and some reworked in the 17th century so as to imitate the original items. The atrium also provides a view of the two bell towers flanking the façade, the

2

Basilica of
Sant'Ambrogio,
aerial view

Basilica of
Sant'Ambrogio,
view of the interior

Campanile dei Monaci on the right being the older (9th century) and the *Campanile dei Canonici* (circa 1128) on the left being more slender in its proportions and decorated with thin strips of stonework. The belfry at the top was built in 1889. Above the narthex (the section of the porch next to the façade) is a great loggia with sloping arches that constitutes the most original feature of the entire construction. Of the three portals providing access to the church, only the central one retains its original sculptural decoration, the reliefs on those at the sides being stylistic imitations.

The interior is divided into three aisles and presents a central section of double height with women's galleries opening onto it. The majestic whole is animated by the uninterrupted succession of great arches set at two levels and cadenced by the alternation of pillars of different height and section. The harmony of the design – the fruit of the experience of the artificers of Milanese Romanesque architecture, which attained full maturity in the 11th century – is underscored by the elegant combination of the cornices of the hanging arches, the slender half columns with carved capitals and the arched lintels of terracotta.

Attention should be drawn on the left to an isolated column crowned with a bronze serpent (possibly of Byzantine workmanship) and the monumental ambo or pulpit, rebuilt with some of the original materials after being destroyed in 1196 by the collapse of a section of the vaulted

2

ceiling adjoining the dome. The base consists of a Roman sarcophagus surrounded by ancient columns decorated with animals and plant motifs. The balustrade is made up of marble panels, the one facing the altar being decorated with a carved depiction of the *Last Supper*. The two metal sculptures on the side looking onto the nave date from the 8th or 9th century. The 9th-century ciborium standing in the last section of the central aisle over the burial place of Saint Ambrose and the martyrs Gervase and Protase consists of four porphyry columns from the classical era supporting four pointed pediments with stucco decorations. The ciborium protects an altar of the Carolingian period adorned on its four sides with panels of silver and gold in frames studded with precious stones and enamel. The scenes depicted include episodes from the lives of Christ and Saint Ambrose. Two medallions on the rear side show Ambrose crowning Angilberto, the archbishop who commissioned the work, and Volvinius, the mysterious craftsman who made the altar. The walls in the area of the apse, which is the oldest part, were restored in the 19th century to the hypothetical simplicity of their Romanesque form. The semi-dome is adorned with a large mosaic, where sections from the 4th and 8th century alternate with others that have been completely remade. It shows *Christ Pantokrator* in the centre and the *Miracle of Saint Ambrose* whereby Saint Ambrose was simultaneously present at a mass in Milan (on the right) and the funeral of the bishop Martin in Tours (on the left). The stone bishop's throne dates from the 9th century and the wooden choir stalls, with polychromatic inlay and intaglio decorations depicting episodes in the life of the saint, are 15th-century work. An ark containing the remains of the patron saints can be seen in the crypt together with the ancient sarcophagus of porphyry in which their bodies were found during the investigations carried out in the 19th century.

The side chapels, all of which date from after the Romanesque period, house some interesting works of art, including frescoes by Giovanni Battista Tiepolo (second chapel on the left) and by Bergognone (first on the right). The wrought-iron gate and atrium at the end of the right aisle provide access to the **Shrine of San Vittore in Ciel d'Oro**. All that survives of the original structure, which dates from the 4th-century and was rebuilt in the 20th century, is the domed roof covered with mosaics depicting saints. Remains of the ancient Christian burial ground that once occupied this site can also be seen in the crypt. The **Museum** holds some of the basilica's treasures in the shape of precious objects produced by Milanese goldsmiths.

The door in the left aisle leads into the **Portico dei Canonici**, where Bramante worked on a cloister commissioned by Ludovico Sforza, a project that was never completed. The building was destroyed during the bombing in 1943 and the two present-day wings were built in its place. This area was occupied in medieval times by a group of build-

2

Volvinio, *Altar of Gold*, main front Basilica of Sant'Ambrogio

ings connected with the basilica and laid out around three courtyards. These were demolished in the first half of the 20th century in order to isolate the church and highlight its monumental status. The sole survivor is the **Oratory of San Sigismondo**, an ancient structure subjected to repeated rebuilding, most recently during the construction of the two wings of the portico. From here we can proceed into Largo Gemelli and enjoy a view of the apse and the structure encasing the dome in its present state after the elements added by Carlo Borromeo were removed in the 19th century. It now presents two tiers of graceful galleries beneath a cornice of hanging arches.

The Monastery of Sant'Ambrogio was suppressed in 1797 and the **Università Cattolica del Sacro Cuore**, founded in 1921, now occupies the site where it once stood. The university complex was designed by Giovanni Muzio and built over the 1930s and 1940s so as to incorporate the remains of the ancient monastery in their 'original' form – with the masonry restored and all later additions removed – into the new structures required for academic functions and purposes. The monastery was originally designed by Donato Bramante with four cloisters but only two were actually built, namely the Ionic cloister on the right and the Doric on the left, which was completed in the 17th century on the basis of the original plans. These still survive together with the Baroque atrium, the staircase and the refectory with frescoes by Callisto Piazza, which is now used as the main hall.

Saint Ambrose, 5th century Basilica of Sant'Ambrogio Sacello di San Vittore in Ciel d'Oro

Muzio combined these ancient structures with a series of buildings to house lecture halls, accommodation facilities, the canteen and the psychology department. Partly facing onto Via Necchi, these structures display the characteristic elements of his architectural vocabulary, including terracotta or clinker facings and the use of exposed brick and stone as quality materials to underscore divisions and members. The influence of the Rationalist school is shown in his later phase by the almost complete abandonment of decoration, a return to classical models and the use of large expanses of glass. The **Chapel of the Sacred Heart**, located between the entrance block and the apse of the basilica, is embellished with sculptures and reliefs by Giacomo Manzù.

Università Cattolica del Sacro Cuore, cloister

Leaving Piazza Sant'Ambrogio by way of Via San Vittore, we find the **Leonardo da Vinci Museum of Science and Technology** housed in the old Olivetan Monastery of San Vittore on the left side of the street. The surviving elements of the religious complex comprise the two cloisters – the first distinguished in particular by its grace and elegance – and the dining hall as well as a significant group of frescoes from different periods by various hands. These are incorporated into the structures erected from 1949 on to repair damage incurred during the war and can thus be seen inside the museum itself. Adjoining the original elements are an aeronautic-naval pavilion and a railway pavilion, near which the sub-

marine *Enrico Toti*, launched in 1967, was installed in 2007 after the mobilisation of means and manpower on a massive scale to transport it from the sea to Milan. Great interest attaches to the Gallery of Machines produced on the basis of the manuscript designs of Leonardo da Vinci and the items in the Transport Section, including a brig, the bridge of an ocean liner and about twenty railway engines and carriages. Situated adjacent to the museum on the right is the **Church of San Vittore al Corpo**, adjoining the monastery and probably founded in the 8th century on the site of the imperial mausoleum. The renovation work commenced by the Olivetan monks in 1560 was completed in 1602, giving the church its present-day appearance. Behind the unfinished façade, the late 16th-century interior is practically intact together with the original decorations and furnishings, including the white and gold stuccowork and the frescoes by Ercole Procaccini on the barrel-vaulted ceiling. Attention should be drawn to the two rows of inlaid wooden choir stalls.

Having returned to Corso Magenta by way of Via Carducci, we can pause at number 36 to admire the **Palazzo Viviani Cova** (1915), a splendid example of the characteristic historicist architecture of the Coppedé brothers, who often drew inspiration from medieval fortress-

Leonardo da Vinci Museum of Science and Technology, porticoed courtyard

2

Casa degli Atellani
(Atellani Family
House), vestibule

Following pages
Santa Maria
delle Grazie

es. The building at number 62 on the stretch of Corso Magenta lead-ing to the Church of Santa Maria delle Grazie is the **Palazzo delle Stelline**, which takes its name from the Benedictine Convent of San-ta Maria della Stella that stood there in the 15th century. Built in the 17th century and now municipal property, it houses a conference cen-tre, among other things. It is made up of three cloisters and includes splendid grounds that are open to visitors. Built by Piero Portaluppi in the 1920s with a revival of 15th-century forms and a Renaissance layout, the **Atellani Family House** stands a little further along on a site known as the Vineyard of Leonardo, some traces of which remain in its grounds. The artist lived here in the old house at the time of the *Last Supper* and this was the location of his beloved vineyard, a gift from Ludovico Sforza on completion of the painting.

Facing onto the piazza of the same name a little way up the street, the Dominican **Church of Santa Maria delle Grazie** was designed by Guiniforte Solari and built over the period from 1465 to 1482. The layout of three aisles with side chapels and groin vaulting is character-istic of the late Gothic Lombard architecture exemplified in Solari's work. The exterior presented two-colour decorations in white plaster and ter-racotta and a broad gabled façade. Having decided to make the church

71

his family mausoleum, Ludovico Sforza ordered some major structural alterations in 1492 and called Bramante in to replace Solari's presbytery with a new apse. It was also in this connection that Ludovico commissioned Leonardo da Vinci to paint the celebrated *Last Supper* that adorns the refectory. Ludovico's great plans, which also included rebuilding the façade and aisles, were never put fully into effect, as work ceased after the completion of the apse, the sacristy and the *Last Supper*. Despite the changes and the damage incurred in the bombing of 1943, which destroyed the library and the Chiostro dei Morti (Cloister of the Dead), these works still give a very significant idea of the splendour of Milan under the Sforza dynasty. Bramante's apse is seen from the outside as a combination of rigorously geometric forms that continues the two-colour scheme (white and terracotta) of the existing building and enriches it with decorative elements typical of the Lombard tradition. The structure consists of a cube-shaped volume with a semicircular recess on either side beneath a dome mounted on a polygonal drum. The marble entrance in the centre of the façade is also generally attributed to Bramante.

Inside, the apse opens up at the end of the nave as a light-filled space on a grand scale with cornices and edges marking out the geometry of the architectural elements and walls decorated with simple graffito motifs. The ceilings of the side aisles are frescoed, as are the tympanums of the central aisle, which present figures of saints. Among the altarpieces and frescoes of the 16th, 17th and 18th centuries in the side chapels, attention should be drawn to the *Scenes of the Passion* attributed to Gaudenzio Ferrari (fourth chapel on the right) and a *Holy Family* by Paris Bordon (sixth on the left). The first chapel on the left holds a *Crucifixion* and six bas-reliefs by Francesco Messina (1981). By proceeding through a chapel and a sacristy at the end of the left aisle, we can reach the **Chiostrino**, the last of the three cloisters that originally made up the Dominican convent. It has traditionally been regarded as the work of Bramante. An inlaid door on the side facing the apse is the entrance to the **Old Sacristy**. The ceiling of the great apsidal hall is decorated with a motif of knotted ropes in the Leonardesque style.

In order to enter the **Refectory** and see Leonardo's *Last Supper* we must return to the piazza and go through an 18th-century atrium into a large rectangular hall dating from Solari's building. The wall opposite Leonardo's work is decorated with a fresco of the *Crucifixion* by Giovanni Donato Montorfano (1495), to which the figures of Ludovico Sforza and Beatrice d'Este with their children were added in tempera. Now practically invisible, these portraits may have been the work of Leonardo. Taking Via Caradosso, which runs to the rear of Santa Maria delle Grazie, we arrive at **Piazzale Cadorna** and the North Milan Railway Sta-

Donato Bramante, interior of the dome of Santa Maria delle Grazie

Pages 78–79
Piazzale Cadorna with the sculpture *Needle, Thread and Knot* by Claes Oldenburg and Coosje van Bruggen, 2000

tion. This square was renovated together with the façade of the station in 2000 within the framework of a project developed by Gae Aulenti. Elements of this can be seen in the canopy of steel and iron resting on columns in front of the building and the sculpture *Needle, Thread and Knot* by Claes Oldenburg and Coosje van Bruggen, which crosses the square, going underground like the trains of the subway system, and pays an imaginative tribute both to the hard-working Milanese and above all to the world of fashion.

Via Monti and Via Boccaccio lead from Piazzale Cadorna into the **Magenta district**, built in the late 19th and early 20th century on the ba-

Leonardo da Vinci's
Last Supper

The Last Supper was painted between 1494 and 1497 within the framework of the major renovation of the Monastery of Santa Maria delle Grazie commenced by order of Ludovico Sforza in 1492. Instead of fresco, the normal Renaissance technique for wall paintings, Leonardo used tempera on a dry wall, which gave him the greatest possible freedom to alter and correct the composition while the work was in progress and enabled him to obtain particular effects of colour. It is, however, partly as a result of this choice that the painting is now in a very poor state of preservation. Although the Last Supper – a representation of the Eucharist – was a subject traditionally depicted in the refectories of monasteries, especially in Florence, Leonardo took a radically innovative approach with marked accentuation of the dramatic elements of the scene.

Christ's announcement to the disciples that one of them will betray him causes reactions of shock and astonishment, typical instances of the 'motions of the mind' that Leonardo investigated with such interest in his studies. In a setting of extraordinarily exact perspective, which seems to suggest that the scene is taking place inside the refectory of the Dominican monks in Milan, colour is used to define the effects of the light entering both from the three windows in the background and from the real one in the room. Previously distorted by attempts at restoration carried out over the centuries, Leonardo's original painting has now emerged as a result of the work begun in 1978 and completed in 1999.

This involved addressing complex problems as regards not only the painting itself but also the environment of the refectory in order to protect the work from the dust, fumes and humidity identified as the primary causes of its constant deterioration.

Leonardo da Vinci,
The Last Supper,
1497
Convent of Santa
Maria delle Grazie

Casa Donzelli
(Donzelli House),
detail of the loggia-
style balcony and
tripartite windows
Via Gioberti 1

sis of the city's planning scheme of 1884. While architecturally varied, it is of interest above all for the numerous buildings in the Art Nouveau style known in Italy as Liberty scattered among more traditional works of an eclectic character as evidence of the readiness of Milan's middle classes to embrace modernism. The **Casa Donzelli** by Ulisse Stacchini (1903–1904) at Via Gioberti 1 is one of the first and most interesting works of this kind and presents a graceful linear structure with loggia-style balconies and ceramic decorations with bright floral motifs. A short detour to the right will take us to the **Casa Bosisio** at Via Saffi 9, which presents a ceramic facing with bunches of sunflowers together with decorative elements of concrete and wrought iron. Interest also attaches to the **Case Maffioretti** at numbers 12 and 14. Again built by Stacchini, the second **Casa Donzelli**, at number 8 in Via Tasso, abandons floral decoration for motifs inspired by the Viennese Secession, as can be seen in the wrought ironwork by Alessandro Maz-

Casa Laugier
(Laugier House)
Corso Magenta 96

2

zucotelli. The **Casa Cavalli Agostoni** at Via Ariosto 21 has a façade decorated with female figures in relief and a fine staircase based on Victor Horta's Art Nouveau models. Located on Piazzale Baracca at the intersection with Corso Magenta, the **Casa Laugier** (1905), designed by Antonio Tagliaferri, develops a sophisticated contrast between concrete, red brick and ceramic tiles with Viennese Secession motifs analogous to those of the wrought ironwork. The celebrated Santa Teresa Pharmacy on the corner still preserves its original Liberty furnishings intact.

From Piazza Buonarroti to the Portello:
The Great Architectures of the 21st Century

3

This itinerary unfolds across the north-western quadrant of the city, an area which up until the pre-war period served as a railway junction, surrounded by cultivated fields and a few neo-medieval villas with gardens, which are still visible between the large residential buildings, chiefly from the post-war period. Starting from the early 20th century, the hosting of the new Fiera Campionaria (Trade Fair) in the former Piazza d'Armi – military parade ground – boosted the development of the surrounding area, for the most part a middle-class, residential district.

At the intersection of Piazza Buonarroti we find a stop of metro line M1. The station, like all others along this line, was designed by Franco Albini and Franca Helg in partnership with graphic designer Bob Noorda. In 1963 these architects envisaged a pioneering system capable of integrating architectural, graphic and décor elements through a modern, avant-garde style.

The project brought Noorda international acclaim, so much so that he was commissioned to design the signs for the metros in New York and São Paulo.

We pass the monument to Giuseppe Verdi and Camillo Boito's neo-medieval Casa di Riposo per Musicisti (Rest Home for Musicians) on our left, and come to a large boulevard, **Via Michelangelo Buonarroti**. Following it all the way down to the corner with **Piazza Giulio Cesare**, we find a notable example of early 20th-century architecture, the **Columbus Nursing Home** (1911–1913), formerly Villa Faccanoni-Romeo, an Art Nouveau building by Giuseppe Sommaruga.

Casa di Riposo per Musicisti Giuseppe Verdi, designed by Camillo Boito

The villa consists of over thirty rooms spread across three floors, a large lodge and a spacious garden (2,300 square metres). The side façade is adorned by two sculptures of female nudes by Ernesto Bazzaro, brought here from Palazzo Castiglioni in Corso Venezia. The palace had earned the nickname of *Ca' di ciapp* (**House of Buttocks**) because of the two sculptures, which had caused quite a stir at the time of its construction (1903).

Rendering of the Three Towers of CityLife

Following pages
View of the residential buildings designed by Zaha Hadid

When the villa was converted into a clinic, the renovation and enlargement of the building were assigned to Gio Ponti and Eugenio Soncini (1938–1940), who continued their work also in the post-war period.

The L-shaped plan of the new wing is marked by a carefully designed functional distribution intended to make patients feel 'at home', as is suggested by the furnishing and equipment created by the designers: each room has a small south-facing balcony that overlooks the large garden of the villa. Leaving the clinic behind, we make our way across Piazza Giulio Cesare and find ourselves facing the **Fountain of the Four Seasons**. Designed by Renzo Gerla in 1927, it now marks a new gateway to one of the city's greatest urban development projects. Following the relocation of most of the Trade Fair district to the new Rho-Pero centre, designed by Massimiliano Fuksas, the area cleared – a surface of roughly 255,000 square metres – became the site of the new **CityLife** neighbourhood. This mixed project by Zaha Hadid, Arata Isozaki and Daniel Libeskind features several residential complexes, three office skyscrapers, a park and other green areas.

The heart of the project is the large square, providing a range of public services, such as the new station for metro line M5 and a network of commercial venues, dominated by the **Three Towers** designed by Zaha Hadid, Arata Isozaki and Daniel Libeskind.

The first tower, by architect Arata Isozaki, stands at a height of 202 metres across fifty floors. Modelled after Constantin Brancusi's *Endless Column*, it represents a metaphor for a mode of construction that knows no limits in its aspiration to reach the sky.

The second tower, by architect Zaha Hadid, stands on the left at a height of 170 metres across forty-four floors. It vertically unfolds with a dynamic twist that enhances one's perception of it viewed against the urban axes.

The third tower, by architect Daniel Libeskind, stands at the centre, rising to approximately 150 metres in height. It was conceived as part of an ideal sphere enveloping the new **Piazza Tre Torri**.

To the right of the large tower by Isozaki are the sinuous residences designed by Zaha Hadid, with façades 'in relief'. Located at the edge of the existing city, they overlook the park on one side and Via Senofonte-Piazza Giulio Cesare on the other.

Daniel Libeskind's residences are situated on the south-western side of the area. They too overlook the park on one side and Via Spinola-Piazza Giulio

Cesare on the other. The CityLife project centres on the development of one of the largest pedestrian areas in Europe, with exclusively underground traffic routes and car parks, and the third largest park in Milan (170,000 square metres), conceived by the Gustafson Porter studio in partnership with !melk and One Works.

Not far from here, on the edge of the old Trade Fair district, the blocks originally designed for the International Exhibition of 1906 were reconverted in the pre-war and post-war period with the development of a densely populated residential area, a project that involved the masters of Milanese architecture of the period.

Architects Mario Asnago and Claudio Vender designed three residential buildings. The first, the **Santa Rita Rental House** (1937–1938), is located on the corner between Via Euripide and Viale Cassiodoro. The central theme of the project was the relation of the new housing block with the street front and pre-existing buildings: the front is slightly curved, creating a degree of continuity between the two façades overlooking the street. The modern quality of this building lies in its simple lines: the aligned openings were given a different treatment on each floor, in such a way as to distinguish the six floors of the rental house. The **Residential Building** (1952–1956) at the crossroads between Via Senofonte, Via Plutarco and Via Pompeo is instead the most unusual building to have been designed by the two architects in the post-war

3

period. It features a complex juxtaposition of openings, deep, inclined loggias, and windows of different sizes with wooden or aluminium frames. The proportions of the street front vary, as this has been designed by the two architects in such a way as to create an alternation of volumes.

Gio Ponti found himself operating with Antonio Fornaroli and Eugenio Soncini on the other block, the one now facing the Libeskind residences. In Via Brin he created the **Casa Laporte** (1935–1938), which may be regarded as the great Milanese master's take on the Rationalist style of the 1930s. The building is on three floors; the simple lines of the windows, the small doorway and the roof garden on the last floor recall Le Corbusier's architecture.

We now leave this area and head towards Piazza Amendola. Here, in addition to one of the finest stations on metro line M1, with a glass-roofed mezzanine, at the crossroads with Via Domenichino and Via Monterosa we find the wonderful Pompeian red building designed by Gio Ponti together with Emilio Lancia in 1928–1931. Conceived for the haute bourgeoisie of Milan, it presents a distinctive corner, dominated by the lantern at the top of the building, with decorative elements stripped down to the minimum through an interplay of white lines and small arches against a red background. Continuing down Via Monterosa, almost on the corner with Piazzale Lotto we find the **Sole24Ore Headquarters**,

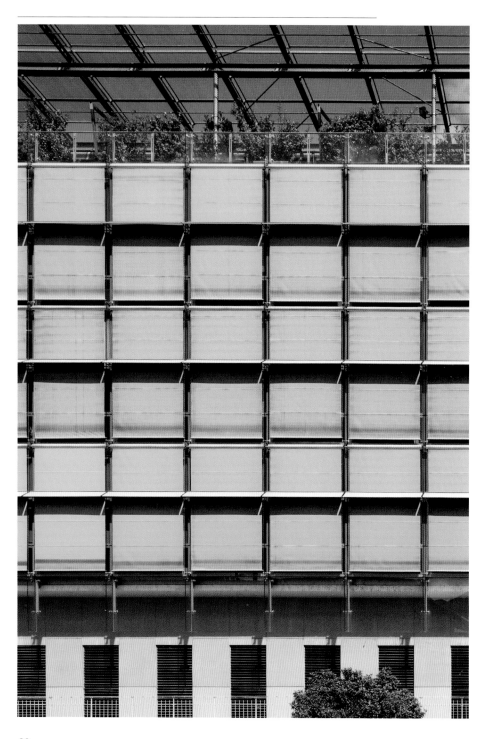

Detail of the façade
of the Sole24Ore
Headquarters

The roof of the
MiCo congress
centre, designed by
Mario Bellini

Following pages
The Sole24Ore
Headquarters,
designed by Renzo
Piano

designed by the Italian architect Renzo Piano. The project for the headquarters of this leading publishing group began with the renovation and raising of a pre-existing U-shaped industrial complex. This unobtrusive yet technologically and structurally highly complex work was carried out by alternating glass walls with a double-layered of ceramic material. In the large courtyard, the architect has created a green mound with, beneath it, the canteen, car park and halls. The main, double-height hall of the complex overlooks the mound. At street level, the entrance is on Via Monterosa.

In this constantly changing part of Milan one last visit should be made to the new Portello district, sprung from the ashes of the former Alfa Romeo plant, which was relocated outside the city in the 1960s.

Strolling down Viale Scarampo, we come across the last remaining fair pavilions, with the large 'tympanum' overlooking the motorway. These buildings were designed by architect Mario Bellini in the mid-1990s and in recent years have partly been converted into the MiCo congress centre, a new landmark in the area. The large silver 'comet' crowning the entrance offers a striking view, particularly at night time.

A little further on is the new Portello district, initially developed in the 1980s. After many ups and downs, the project was finally entrusted to Studio Valle, which drew up the master plan. Here three sail-shaped office buildings by Studio Valle mark the access to Milan from the north. Together with the large fan-shaped plaza designed by the Berlin-based

3

firm TOPOTEK1, these buildings are connected to the rest of the re-developed area by a bridge (designed by the Arup studio), which leads across Viale Serra to the residences by architect Guido Canali. A large park of 70,000 square metres, conceived by the great American plan-ner and architectural theorist Charles Jencks (together with Andreas Kipar/Land and Margherita Brianza), reconnects the whole area to the rest of the city. At one end of the park are the interesting residences by Cino Zucchi, inspired by the apartment buildings designed by leading Milanese masters in the post-war period. The **Portello Park** offers a journey across present, past and future that ends on the edge of the city.

95

The New Expo Complex in the Rho-Pero Area

The building of a new Expo Complex forms part of the large-scale programme of redevelopment for disused areas in the outlying areas and hinterland of Milan. The unified structure designed by Massimiliano Fuksas is organised around a central axis and very simple in form. The main offices and conference centres are located in the middle of the area with the display pavilions at the sides.

As a whole, the structure shows close attention to both functional and aesthetic values. There are façades of reflecting metal, pools of water, green areas, an elevated footbridge and a monumental undulating roof of glass and steel over one kilometre in length recalling natural phenomena like waves and dunes.

From Piazza del Duomo to Porta Ticinese:
The Basilicas, the Canals and the Ancient Suburbs

4

This itinerary runs through the southern part of the city to the lively, bustling area of the canals and the Porta Ticinese district with their shops, clubs and fashionable galleries. The major monuments of ecclesiastical architecture taken in along the way include the Churches of San Satiro with the trompe-l'œil choir by Bramante, San Lorenzo and Sant'Eustorgio with the Portinari Chapel.

Via Torino starts from the southwest corner of Piazza del Duomo (Itinerary 1). Only minimally affected by the 19th-century changes in urban layout, this important commercial thoroughfare marks the starting point of one of the main highways leading from the heart of the city towards the ring of fortifications. This was once the way to the old city gate known as the Porta Ticinese. A short detour to the right along Via Spadari can be made at the beginning in order to take in some interesting buildings in the Italian Art Nouveau style known as Liberty, in particular the **Casa Ferrario** (numbers 3 and 5) with its splendid wrought ironwork of floral and animal motifs by Alessandro Mazzucotelli.

After returning to Via Torino, we arrive at the **Church of Santa Maria presso San Satiro** in a recessed area a little way along on the left. It was built in the late 15th century by an ancient shrine of the Carolingian era dedicated to Saint Satyrus and connected with the destroyed basilica founded in the 9th century by the archbishop Ansperto. The new edifice was dedicated to Our Lady in honour of a miraculous image installed there, which is traditionally held to have shed blood on being stabbed. (This 13th-century painting can be seen inside the church.) The work was entrusted to Donato Bramante, who created the celebrated trompe-l'œil choir that can be seen inside. While the general layout of its floor plan and elevations remains intact, the church was subjected to major alterations in the 19th century, including transformation of the

Church of Santa Maria presso San Satiro, view of the structure encasing the dome and the bell tower

façade, raising of the floor, restructuring of the dome, a complete new decorative scheme with frescoes and gilding on the pilasters, cornices and architraves, and a coffered ceiling in place of the barrel vaulting. The floor plan takes the shape of a cross with three arms of equal length and the fourth on the side with the presbytery missing due to the presence of a street, leaving Bramante no space for the choir. The clean break of a sheer wall would, however, have made it impossible to achieve the harmonious balance of volumes required by the dome and the huge transept. The architect therefore devised a virtual space by means of a bas-relief in coloured terracotta based on the rules of perspective. While actually about 90 centimetres in depth, the structure creates the illusion of a choir with three arches, broad barrel vaulting and rich decoration, similar to the one painted by Piero della Francesca in the *Brera Altarpiece* (Itinerary 7). The images of the *Evangelists* in the spandrels of the dome are all that remains of the church's ancient pictorial ornamentation.

Church of Santa Maria presso San Satiro, choir by Donato Bramante

The baptistery or sacristy to the right of the entrance was also designed by Bramante but largely rebuilt in the 19th century. The trabeation in the upper part is adorned with a frieze of *putti* and male busts sculpted to the architect's drawings by Agostino de' Fondulis, who also worked on the sculptural group from which the shrine of Saint Satyrus takes its name as the **Chapel of the Pietà**. The other distinctive features of this small room opening onto the left arm of the transept are reused capitals from different eras, traces of frescos in the Byzantine style and a small cupola erected during renovation in the 15th century. The intensely dramatic *Pietà* consists of 14 statues of polychromatic terracotta. A good view of the exterior of the church with the two Renaissance portals, the 15th-century structure encasing the dome and the medieval bell tower can be obtained from Via Falcone at the rear.

The **Municipal Temple of Saint Sebastian** further down the street on the right was built by the city as a thanksgiving for the end of the plague in 1576. Designed by Carlo Borromeo's architect Pellegrino Tibaldi, it is an uncompromising example of late-Renaissance Milanese architecture and its insistence on application of the formal classical code. The original design was for a round, two-storey building but various changes made during the long period of construction led to the present structure of a square presbytery with a small 18th-century dome grafted onto a large round structure in three sections, the one in the middle being distinguished by buttresses. The interior includes works ranging from the 17th to the 20th century with a significant group of late 17th-century Lombard paintings.

A little further on, we take a short detour along Via Valpetrosa to see the **Casa dei Grifi** and its 16th-century portico with marble medallions in relief and grotesques at number 5. Returning to Via Torino, we then

INRI

IMPONVNT PLECTENTES CORONAM SPINEAM

ET FLAGEL
LAVIT EVM

ECCE
HOMO

4

Church of
Sant'Alessandro,
façade

Bernardino Luini,
*Scenes from the
Passion*, 1516
San Giorgio al
Palazzo

take Via della Palla on the left into a small square with the 18th-century Palazzo Trivulzio and the 17th-century **Church of Sant'Alessandro** forming part of the adjacent Barnabite college. The work on the latter began in 1601 to designs by Lorenzo Binago based on those by Bramante and Michelangelo for Saint Peter's in Rome, hence the breadth of the façade flanked by two towers and the central plan in the form of two juxtaposed Greek crosses. After various stages of construction maintaining a complete uniformity of style that makes Sant'Alessandro the most coherent example of Baroque religious architecture in Milan, the building was completed in 1710 with the addition of the contrasting Rococo forms of the upper section of the façade. The 17th-century furnishings and decorations of the interior remain intact, with paintings by Filippo Abbiati, Federico Bianchi, Camillo Procaccini and Daniele Crespi. Attention should also be drawn to the confessionals of carved wood and marble and the sumptuous high altar (1641) inlaid with precious stonework and gems.

Continuing once again along Via Torino, we come to another important church where the road widens on the right, namely **San Giorgio al Palazzo**, whose name recalls the fact that all this area as far as the Piazza del Duomo was once occupied by the late-Roman imperial palace. Its present appearance is the result of various episodes of restoration in the 18th and 19th centuries. The interior is neoclassical in style and there is a series of works by Bernardino Luini illustrating episodes from the Passion (1516) in the third chapel on the right. Turning left down Via Soncino, we then arrive at the 19th-century façade of **Palazzo Stampa di Soncino** (number 2), a 16th-century edifice dominated by a tower that tapers in sections and bears the symbols of Charles V on two columns. The fine courtyard has a two-storey portico.

Just before the Carrobbio (a corruption of *quadrivium*, the Latin word for a crossroads), Via San Sisto leads to the deconsecrated church of the same name that houses the **Francesco Messina Studio and Museum** with works of the artist (1900–1995). Sicilian by birth but Milanese by adoption, this celebrated sculptor was personally responsible for restoring the building, which was his studio for many years, and bequeathed a collection of drawings and over 80 sculptures to the city. Interest attaches in particular to a group of splendid portraits and the series of bronzes depicting female dancers and horses.

Palazzo Stampa di Soncino, view of the west façade on Via Soncino

The itinerary then continues along Corso di Porta Ticinese, an area occupied in medieval times by a bustling suburban neighbourhood with a host of artisan's workshops known as *Cittadella*. This part of the city was subjected to radical changes starting in the 19th century. The covering over of the canals and severe bombing in World War II have left little trace of the ancient fabric. The first stretch takes us as far as the intersection with Via Gian Giacomo Mora and the point where the column referred to in the title of Manzoni's *Storia della colonna infame* (Story of the Infamous Column) once stood. Demolished in the late 18th century, the column commemorated an appalling episode in 1630, when the barber Gian Giacomo Mora, who lived on that very spot, was accused of spreading the plague and executed. A little further along on the left

4

View of the apse
of San Lorenzo
Maggiore with the
Parco delle
Basiliche

Following pages
Colonnade and
Basilica of San
Lorenzo Maggiore

we come to the **Basilica of San Lorenzo Maggiore** preceded by its celebrated colonnade of 16 columns from a building of the classical era that formed part of the now destroyed quadriporticus in front of the basilica in ancient times. Comprising the central nucleus of the church proper and three satellite buildings, the basilica was built in the late 4th and early 5th century. The lack of definitively established information about its foundation has given rise to various hypotheses, including the particularly intriguing claim that it was built by an emperor as his mausoleum, possibly within the context of the clash between orthodox Catholicism and the Arian heresy, which flourished at the imperial court of Milan. While the façade is the result of restoration in the 19th century, the interior gives a clear idea of the layout of the ancient edifice, which was respectfully preserved during the two phases of rebuilding necessitated by fire and collapse, one in medieval times and the other in the late 16th century. The theme of the central plan is repeated with variations throughout the complex, the main church consisting in particular of a square

structure surrounded by four columned semi-circular recesses and four square corner towers connected with one another by an ambulatory. Filled with light and dynamic in structure, the edifice conveys the awesome solemnity of late imperial art. Its austere appearance, emphasized by the way the members stand out against the sober grey of the bare stone, can be regarded as the result of the 16th-century restoration undertaken by Martino Bassi for Carlo Borromeo. Restricted in his freedom of action by the survival of part of the outer walls of the ancient building, the architect focused essentially on solving the problem of the dome, which had collapsed in 1573. Greater in diameter than that of the Cathedral, this structure rests on a tall octagonal drum. The early Christian building must be imagined as entirely covered in mosaics and not unlike the Basilica of San Vitale in Ravenna, for which it may have provided a model. There are frescoes from different periods between the 12th and the 17th centuries on the walls of the ambulatory and the smaller chapels. The largest of the three buildings adjoining the main church – all of which are centrally focused and symmetrical in plan – is the **Chapel of Sant'Aquilino** to the right of the entrance. A small atrium adorned with

Christ with the Apostles
Basilica of San Lorenzo Maggiore, Chapel of Sant'Aquilino

the remains of 4th-century mosaics and a fine Roman portal provide access to the edifice, which is traditionally regarded as having been built for Galla Placidia, the daughter of the Emperor Theodosius and better known for her Mausoleum in Ravenna. The sarcophagus on the right is said to be hers. A series of 16th-centuries frescoes provides a background for two splendid early Christian mosaics depicting *Christ with the Apostles* and the *Ascent of Elijah*, which were part of the now lost original decoration. Interest also attaches to the other two chapels, the earlier one being dedicated to Saint Hippolytus and the other to Saint Sixtus.

Piazza Vetra at the rear of the complex offers the best view of the exterior, making it possible to distinguish the early Christian structure in brick and the 16th-century dome and drum as well as the adjoining chapels. The **Parco delle Basiliche** (Park of the Basilicas) starts here and forms a link also in visual terms between the apse of San Lorenzo and the Basilica of Sant'Eustorgio at the end of the avenue. Returning onto the main road, we continue as far as the medieval city gate known as the **Porta Ticinese**. Together with the arches of the Porta Nuova, this is the only surviving element of the 11th-century walls, which were then

expanded in the era of Spanish rule. Its present-day appearance, including the picturesque Guelph battlements, is the result of the restoration work carried out in the 19th century by Camillo Boito, one of the first in a whole series of operations on the city's ancient monuments. We then turn right down Via De Amicis to reach the area of the Roman arena and proceed from there to the Church of San Vincenzo in Prato.

The **Park of the Roman Amphitheatre** and the **Alda Levi Antiquarium** (Via De Amicis 17) includes some stretches of the radial walls of the ancient Milanese arena (1st and 2nd century), which stood outside the city walls and was destroyed in the 6th century at the time of the Gothic invasion. Materials from the amphitheatre were used in the construction of the Basilica of San Lorenzo. Among other things, the Antiquarium includes an educational section devoted to reconstructions of the types of combat and spectacle staged in the amphitheatre. We turn from Via De Amicis into Via Conca dei Navigli, whose name recalls the fact that this was the site of one of the five locks in the canal system making it possible to negotiate differences in level. Part of this structure can still be seen in the tree-lined widening at the end of the road. The nearby **Basilica of**

4

Basilica of
Sant'Eustorgio

San Vincenzo in Prato was probably built in the 11th century on the model of early Christian architecture. Like many other medieval Milanese buildings, the church owes its present appearance to work carried out in the 19th century to restore its original form, also through rebuilding. The 20th-century baptistery is the work of Paolo Mezzanotte.

Having returned to Corso di Porta Ticinese, we now proceed to the **Basilica of Sant'Eustorgio**. Traditionally held to date from the 4th century but possibly later, the church bears identifiable traces of an earlier Romanesque building of the 11th and 12th century in the area of the apse. Established as a Dominican monastery in 1220, Sant'Eustorgio was one of the most important building projects in the Lombard Gothic style. The shape taken by the basilica at the end of the great process of transformation developed in the 13th and 14th centuries was restored – and partly reconstructed – by work carried out in the 19th century and after World War II. Among other things, the monastery was a chapter of the Inquisition and its guests included the friar Pietro da Verona, who was killed in an ambush in 1252. His immediate canonisation as Saint Peter the Martyr and the burial of his remains in the church made Sant'Eustorgio a place

The District of Porta Genova

Starting from Corso Genova and proceeding beyond the railway station of the same name, we enter a district whose industrial past of workers' homes and factories has given way in the last few years to a new role as the dynamically developing hub of artistic and creative activities connected with fashion and communication. Scattered among the bustling cafés, shops and galleries are a number of important landmarks. In Via Bergognone stand the Bergognone 53 complex – with a glass-roofed inner courtyard – and the **Armani Theatre**, which was designed by the Japanese architect Tadao Ando and inaugurated in 2001. The actual theatre may be accessed by walking down a hundred-metre-long corridor. The theatre hall, with a seating capacity for six hundred people, features a luminous removable forestage. The strength of this architecture lies in the 'light' use of concrete made by the Japanese architect through the combination of an endless range of grey hues, clear-cut geometries, and original spatial and lighting solutions.

Armani/Silos opened at number 40 at the end of April 2015. This is the new exhibition space displaying a selection of the famous designer's creations.

In Via Tortona 56, the former Ansaldo plant is now home to the **MuDEC, Museo delle Culture**. Inaugurated in March 2015, the museum is a centre for interdisciplinary research on world cultures. Through the historical and ethnographic collections of the city and collaboration with different resident communities, both in Milan and in their home countries, the museum seeks to establish a dialogue on topics related to visual and performance arts, music, design and social practices. The complex presents an inner façade overlooking a central hall, and a covered plaza designed as a reception area. The double translucent glass façade of the hall has a system of walkways leading to the exhibit areas. The new cultural centre is marked by square-shaped, zinc-plated bodies and a central, permanently lit glass structure that displays a geometry in striking contrast to the surrounding volumes.

Armani Theatre, designed by Tadao Ando

Interior of the MuDEC

4

of great veneration. As a result, bequests and donations poured in from aristocratic families eager for burial in its precincts. In addition to the veneration of Peter the Martyr, the basilica was also point of reference for the cult of the Magi. According to a somewhat controversial tradition, the relics of the Three Wise Men had been held in the church in ancient times before being looted by the Holy Roman Emperor Frederick I, known as Barbarossa, and taken to Cologne. It was here that the procession of the Three Kings stopped on its way through Milan, a custom still documented in the 14th century, and it is precisely to such traditions that Sant'Eustorgio owes its countless artistic treasures, dating above all from the 13th, 14th and 15th centuries. While these are still in place, some of the later furnishings and decoration were instead removed in the 19th century.

God the Father,
circa 1570
Museo Diocesano

The façade was rebuilt in what was regarded as its original style by the 19th-century restorers. The nave has three aisles, each divided into eight bays, and a groin-vaulted ceiling. Some of the capitals of the pillars, which differ in cross-section, date back to the Romanesque building and are decorated with interweaving plant motifs or human and animal figures. The aisle on the right contains a series of chapels built by noble families as from the end of the 13th century and adorned with frescoes and impressive funeral monuments. The first is the Brivio Chapel (1483–1489), which owes its present-day Renaissance form to restoration work and contains a fine triptych by Bergognone as well as a highly sophisticated 15th-century tomb. The outstanding feature of the next chapel is the Funeral Monument of Pietro Torelli with the splendid recumbent figure of its occupant. The fourth chapel, built by the Visconti family, contains a precious wooden Crucifix of intensely dramatic character dating from around the 13th century. The ceiling is decorated with Gothic frescoes of the *Four Evangelists* and the right wall with a courtly scene featuring *Saint George and the Dragon*. The Gothic aedicule with Solomonic (twisting) columns on the same wall is the Funeral Monument of Stefano Visconti. The ceiling of the last chapel, belonging to the Torriani family, was frescoed with saints and the symbols of the evangelists in the 15th century.

The transept has only one arm, which begins at the end of the right aisle and contains the Chapel of the Magi. The colossal late-Roman sarcophagus on the right wall is traditionally supposed to have contained the precious remains looted by Barbarossa. The marble dossal of the high altar in the presbytery may have been a gift from Gian Galeazzo Visconti. It is carved with high-relief decorations representing the *Crucifixion* and eight *Scenes from the Life of Christ*.

The outer wall on the right side of the building is adorned with the small pointed façades of the chapels modelled on the front of the transept and showing slight stylistic variations. The 17th-century cloisters of the monastery situated to the left of the basilica now house the **Diocesan Museum**.

The Portinari Chapel

Behind the apse of Sant'Eustorgio, where the head of Peter the Martyr was once preserved, the Tuscan banker Pigello Portinari had a monumental chapel built to house his own tomb and the precious relic of the saint. The square building with a domed roof was completed by 1468. The name of the architect is not known but some have suggested the hand of a Tuscan master drawing inspiration (possibly at his client's request) from the Old Sacristy by Brunelleschi in the Church of San Lorenzo in Florence. The rich decoration of the chapel is, however, purely Lombard. The cornices, arches, pilasters and capitals – some of terracotta and some stone – are enlivened by the presence of plant motifs, cherubs and busts of saints. Delicate figures of angels dancing and playing musical instruments can be seen on the drum.

The walls are adorned with frescoes by Vincenzo Foppa combining subtle naturalism with the deft use of perspective. Comprising an *Annunciation* and *Scenes from the Life of Peter the Martyr*, one of which is the celebrated depiction of his murder, they are among the greatest masterpieces of 15th-century Lombard painting.
The Ark of Peter the Martyr – which contains the remains of the inquisitor and was commissioned by the friars of Sant'Eustorgio, with the support of Azzone Visconti, from the Pisan sculptor Giovanni di Balduccio – was placed in the centre of the chapel in the 18th century. Completed in 1339, it consists of a sarcophagus of Carrara marble resting on small pillars, each of which stands behind a statue of one of the Virtues.
The sides are adorned with eight panels depicting episodes from the saint's life in relief. The lid is richly adorned with statues beneath a pediment with three pinnacles.

Vincenzo Foppa,
The Miracle of the Cloud, 1468–1470
Basilica of Sant'Eustorgio,
Portinari Chapel

Basilica of Sant'Eustorgio,
view of the interior of the Portinari Chapel with the *Ark of Peter the Martyr*,
1335–1339

4

Inaugurated in 2001, it holds paintings, sculptures and precious objects ranging from the 4th to the 19th century. Particular attention should be drawn to the precious collection of 41 panels with gilded backgrounds of the 14th and 15th century by artists of the Tuscan and Umbrian schools. Proceeding a short distance beyond the church, we arrive at Piazzale XXIV Maggio and the monumental **Porta Ticinese** or Ticino Gate (1801–1814) in the centre, built by Luigi Cagnola to celebrate Napoleon's victory at Marengo. With its noble and austere architecture vocabulary drawing upon classical and Palladian models, this constitutes one of the finest examples of Milanese neoclassicism. Located on the other side of the gate, just outside the Spanish walls, was a suburb that grew up in the 17th century around what is now Corso San Gottardo and consisted of buildings with courtyards on long, narrow sites, which acted as internal roads of a semi-private character. Number 18 provides a good example of this type of residential building, known as a *casa di ringhiera* because the front doors of all the homes open onto the railed walkways visible on the upper floors, the ground floor being traditionally occupied by shops and storerooms. The complex system of suburbs, streets and canals converging in this part of the city had one of its focal points in the **Darsena**, a dock on the west side of Piazzale XXIV Maggio at the point where the two surviving branches of the old canal system meet, namely the **Naviglio Grande**, which stretches for 50 kilometres and connects the city with Abbiategrasso, and the **Naviglio Pavese**, 33 kilometres in length. The Darsena has been the object of a substantial redevelopment project, which envisaged the creation of new embankments, paths and docks for tourist boats, and the renovation of Piazza XXIV Maggio, which was converted into an almost exclusively pedestrian area with green stretches. Trees are being planted along the paths running parallel to the banks of the Darsena, while along its western edge a green area will extend down to the water level. The embankments along the canals (*alzaie*) once served as towpaths but are now the scene of bustling nightlife. A well-known antique market is held on the Naviglio Grande on the last Sunday of every month. Situated at the beginning of the canal, a stretch of which can also be travelled along by boat, is the **Vicolo dei Lavandai**, with public laundry facilities under long wooden canopies. The Gothic **Church of San Cristoforo sul**

4

The Church of San Cristoforo sul Naviglio

Naviglio, located about 1.5 kilometres away, was enlarged by Gian Galeazzo Visconti and holds some important 15th and 16th-century paintings. From Piazzale XXIV Maggio, Viale Gian Galeazzo leads south to the Bocconi University and north to the Church of Santa Maria dei Miracoli presso San Celso. Located on Via Sarfatti, the **Università Commerciale Luigi Bocconi**, an advanced centre of economics and business studies, is a private university of great prestige. The historical buildings of the campus, designed by Pagano and Predeval (1937–1941), provide an interesting example of European Rationalist architecture. Consisting of freely arranged buildings differing in volume and profile, the complex forms a unified whole due to the handling of the façades, whose white surfaces are enlivened by modular doors and windows. The original nucleus, already expanded by Muzio in the 1950s, has recently been joined by a new complex looking onto Viale Bligny and structured like a system of courtyards, bridges, cloisters and corridors. Its design is due to the Grafton Architects studio based in Dublin.

Proceeding along Corso Italia, a road built in the late 19th and early 20th century and lined with some interesting examples of 20th-century architecture, we arrive at the 16th-century **Sanctuary of Santa Maria dei Miracoli**. The complex consists of the church of this name and the earlier Church of San Celso, which stood in medieval times in a village where the Virgin Mary is traditionally supposed to have worked some miracles. The massive influx of pilgrims led to the foundation of the new church, built at the end of the 15th century and subjected to substantial alterations and additions over the following century. The basilica is entered through a quadriporticus looking onto the gardens. A sober masterpiece by Cesare Cesariano dating from the early 16th century, it originally presented a simple facing of exposed brick. The tall and highly ornate façade by Martino Bassi (1572) is decorated with statues, busts and bas-reliefs. The interior, with a three-aisle nave and an apse surrounded by a wide ambulatory, retains the original 16th-century furnishings and decoration with frescoes, statues, inlaid marble and gilding. Attention should be drawn primarily to the wooden choir designed by Galeazzo Alessi (1579) and the main altar by Martino Bassi with its statue of *Our Lady of the Assumption*, an object of intense veneration. The apse, drum and dome constitute the earliest part of the building, dating back to the initial phase of construction in the 15th century. The drum is decorated with stucco friezes by Agostino de' Fondulis. In addition to the paintings by Campi, Cerano, Procaccini, Moretto and Paris Bordon, the altarpiece of the *Madonna and Child with Saints* by Bergognone in the first chapel on the left is also worthy of note.

Founded by Saint Ambrose and rebuilt in the 11th century, the Romanesque **Church of San Celso** can be reached from the right transept. While its bell tower is one of the most ancient in the city, the façade looking onto a delightful enclosed garden was built halfway through the 19th century in the same style as and with some elements from the original, which had been demolished at the beginning of the century together with the first two bays of the building.

Continuing along Corso Italia, but not as far as Piazza Missori (Itinerary 5), we arrive at the **Church of San Paolo Converso**, whose fine façade with marked chiaroscuro contrasts, projecting elements and sculptures was designed by Cerano in 1513. The frescoes by Vincenzo and Antonio Campi inside this deconsecrated church include a series on the ceiling (1586–1589) that use perspective to create remarkable illusionistic effects and constitute one of the most extraordinary examples of 16th-century painting in Milan. The adjacent Church of Sant'Eufemia was almost entirely rebuilt in the 19th century.

4

From Piazza del Duomo to Porta Vittoria: Palazzo Reale and the Great Architectural Works of the Renaissance

5

C overing a large area in the southeast sector of the city before heading north as far as the Città Studi University Complex, this itinerary takes in some major works of Renaissance architecture, such as the Ca' Granda with its celebrated 15th-century façades based on designs by Filarete, the Church of San Nazaro with the 16th-century Trivulzio Mausoleum, and the Church of Santa Maria della Passione, yet another Milanese variation on the theme of Bramante's characteristic central plan and adorned with fine frescoes by Bergognone, among other things. It is also possible to continue southeast outside the city as far as the medieval Abbey of Chiaravalle with its wealth of frescoes from the 15th, 16th and 17th centuries.

The itinerary starts from the **Palazzo Reale** (Royal Palace), which stands to the right of the Cathedral. The Broletto Vecchio stood in this area during the period of the city-state before becoming a residence of the Visconti family. Azzone Visconti had it entirely rebuilt in 1330 but all that remains of this 14th-century edifice is the second of its two courtyards and a few elements on the right side of the building. After the court moved to the Sforza Castle (Itinerary 1), the building became the seat first of the Spanish authorities and then of the Austrian governor, Archduke Ferdinand I, who subjected it to a project of complex and almost total renovation. The work was carried out by Giuseppe Piermarini, who proceeded to demolish the wall closing off the main courtyard on the side opposite the Cathedral (the present-day Piazzetta Reale), gave the façades the new and elegant appearance that can still be seen, and reorganised the interior entirely. This period saw the creation of the atrium, the vestibule, the main staircase and the apartments on the first floor, which were further embellished by Napoleon. Seriously damaged in the bombing of 1943, the losses from which included Andrea Appiani's de-

Palazzo Reale, main staircase

125

Museum of the
20th Century,
view of the interior

pictions of Napoleon's deeds (the *Fasti di Napoleone* series) in the Hall of Caryatids, the building has been restored in recent years and converted to become an important art centre. In addition to rooms for temporary exhibitions, it houses the **Museum of the Cathedral** (Itinerary 1) and the **Museum of the Royal Palace**. Inaugurated in 2002, the latter consists of a series of the building's neoclassical rooms, now visible in all their ancient splendour as the result of restoration and the salvaging of original furnishings. Attention should be drawn to the fine decorations by skilled artists such as the painter Giulio Traballesi and the sculptor Giocondo Albertolli, who based his work on an iconographic programme of allegorical and mythological themes devised with the assistance of the poet Giuseppe Parini.

Originally forming part of the Palazzo Reale complex, the **Church of San Gottardo in Corte** can be reached by crossing the courtyard and going out onto Via Pecorari. Built by Azzone Visconti as a chapel connected with the residence, the 14th-century church has undergone partial destruction and alteration. The elements of the original structure still visible include the apse and the bell tower (by Francesco Pecorari from Cremona), both evidently restored, and the ancient entrance, now shifted to the right side. The interior was transformed into an elegant neoclassical chamber by Giocondo Albertolli but retains some of its Gothic elements in a *Crucifixion* by a painter from the school of Giotto and the mausoleum of Azzone Visconti by the Pisan sculptor Giovanni di Balduccio.

The **Arengario**, one of the twin buildings that come into view on our return to Piazza del Duomo, was erected in the 20th century abutting the 'long wing' of the Palazzo Reale (the one closing off the right side of the small square). Begun in 1939 and designed by a team including Giovanni Muzio and Piero Portaluppi, it is an interesting example of the 'lictorial' architecture of the Fascist regime. It consists of a base with three large rectangular entrances and bas-relief decorations by Arturo Martini supporting a loggia structure with two tiers of round arches reminiscent in its restrained solemnity of Roman monumental architecture. After a long restoration, the Arengario now houses the **Museo del Novecento** (Museum of the 20th Century). Inaugurated in December 2010, the museum houses part of the municipal collection of 20th-century art, consisting of works either purchased by the city council of Milan or donated by artists and collectors, including the Jucker and Boschi-Di Stefano families.

With the restoration of the Arengario and of the second floor of the Palazzo Reale, supervised by architects Italo Rota and Fabio Fornasari, a vertical connection has been established through the creation of a spiral ramp in the Arengario tower, which marks the beginning of the museum itinerary. The chronologically ordered display illustrates the development

127

Giuseppe Pellizza da Volpedo: *The Fourth Estate*

Executed by Pellizza between 1898 and 1901, the painting was purchased by public subscription by the Milan city council in 1920.

Pellizza chose this title, by which the work is now universally known, shortly before submitting it for the first Turin *Quadriennale of 1902, in place of The Path of Workers*. The subject, inspired by a labourers' strike in the painter's home town of Volpedo, in Piedmont, was explored through two earlier versions of the same work: *Ambassadors of Hunger*, executed in 1892, was redeveloped into the more symbolist *Flood* in 1895–1896. The painting, a celebration of Workers' Day (established in Italy in 1891), shows a group of labourers moving forward, led by three full-height figures in the foreground: a man, at the centre, flanked by a second, older worker a little behind him and by a woman with a baby in her arms.

The setting is a sunlit square, closed off by dense vegetation in the background, which also conceals the surrounding architecture, and by a stretch of sky with reddish streaks, enclosed within an arched frame. The three main figures are not arranged on the same line, but in an almost wedge-like formation. Likewise, the figures in the background are only apparently arranged in a row: as their shadows reveal, they actually form a wavy pattern, which is further emphasised by their hand gestures, as well as by the rhythm and direction of their heads. This layout ensures that the painting will not appear static or heavy, suggesting instead an unbroken rhythm which conveys the idea of a march forward. *The Fourth Estate* is a complex work that springs from a mature and highly effective use of colour. On the large canvas, coated with glue and chalk, Pellizza first traced the reference lines required in order to define the position of the various figures across different planes, along with the setting.

At a second stage the painter applied pure colours, with a vast range of hues, distributing dots and lines according to the rules of Divisionism, in such a way as to achieve compelling lighting effects, as well as airiness or density, in his treatment of both landscape and figures.

Giuseppe Pellizza da Volpedo, *The Fourth Estate*, 1901 Museum of the 20th Century

Room of the
Futurists
Museum of the 20th
Century

The staircase
of the Museum
of the 20th Century,
designed by Italo
Rota

5

of 20th-century Italian art from Futurism to Arte Povera. Some monographic rooms focus on artists that have been particularly significant for the city of Milan and its municipal collection, such as Morandi, de Chirico, Arturo Martini and Piero Manzoni. The first work to welcome visitors is *The Fourth Estate*, the large canvas by Pellizza da Volpedo which the city council purchased by public subscription in 1920. On display are roughly 350 out of the almost 4,000 works in the collection. The first room, devoted to the international avant-gardes, is the only one featuring foreign artists, including Picasso, Braque and Kandinsky. The itinerary continues with Umberto Boccioni and the Futurists, the Novecento Italiano movement and the art of the inter-war period, down to the abstractionism of the 1930s, exemplified by a noteworthy group of plaster casts by Fausto Melotti. On the two top floors of the tower, the Lucio Fontana room commands a magnificent view of Piazza Duomo. Past a series of Informal works from the 1950s and 1960s, a walkway connecting the Arengario to the Palazzo Reale leads visitors to discover the art of the following decades: from the environments created by the Gruppo T and Luciano Fabro to Arte Povera installations. One final section is devoted to the collection of the Marino Marini Museum, which was bequeathed to the city in 1973 and is now part of the Museo del Novecento.

From Via Marconi, which separates the Arengario from its twin, we proceed to **Piazza Diaz**, which was built in accordance with the urban-planning scheme of 1934 and includes the INA building by Piero Portaluppi

(1934–1937) at number 6 and a tower block at number 7 that houses the Terrazza Martini, a renowned and highly exclusive nightclub offering a spectacular view of the city. The 20th-century buildings lining the sides of the nearby **Piazza Missori** include works by Giovanni Muzio, Emilio Lancia (number 1) and Marcello Piacentini (the INPS building at number 10). Also facing onto the square is the apse of the Gothic **Church of San Giovanni in Conca**, the ancient mausoleum of the Visconti family. This is all that remains of the church after the demolitions carried out in 1879 in order to build the adjoining Via Mazzini. From here we also have an excellent view of the **Torre Velasca**, a tower block standing in the nearby piazza of the same name. Built in 1956–1958 by the BBPR firm of architects (Banfi, Belgiojoso, Peressutti and Rogers), this was intended to establish a fruitful dialogue with the urban setting and hence became a focal point of debate on the relationship between architecture and the environment. Its particular shape is in fact sup-

The Velasca Tower

posed to capture the 'essence of the history of Milan', eschewing direct citation but drawing inspiration at the same time both from the tower of the Sforza Castle and from the architecture of the Cathedral, whose emphasis on structural elements is reflected in the diagonal elements supporting the upper section and connecting it to the rectangular base.

From Piazza Missori we take Corso di Porta Romana, whose name derives from the fact that it leads to the gate that already connected the city's main axis with the road for Rome as far back as the Augustan era. Standing to the left on the site of the now lost medieval gate is the **Basilica of San Nazaro Maggiore**, founded by Saint Ambrose in 382. It once held the remains of the apostles John, Andrew and Thomas, and was known for this reason as the *Basilica Apostolorum*. Almost entirely destroyed in a great fire in 1075, it was rebuilt in the Romanesque style at the beginning of the 12th century. The marshal Gian Giacomo Trivulzio, lieutenant of Louis XII of France, had a mausoleum built for the Trivulzio family abutting the façade of the basilica in 1511. Leonardo da Vinci was initially to have undertaken the work but the mausoleum was actually designed by Bramantino and presents itself on the outside

Bramantino
(Bartolomeo
Suardi), interior of
the mausoleum of
the Trivulzio family,
1511

5

as an unfinished two-storey block. The octagonal interior is soberly decorated with pilasters and family coats-of-arms. The family tombs rest in large niches on the lower level with fine works of 16th-century sculpture. The tomb of Gian Giacomo is located over the present entrance to the church.

Subjected to repeated rebuilding between the 16th and 20th centuries, the basilica proper maintains the original cross-shaped layout of the Ambrosian church with a single-aisled nave. Apart from the foundations, the surviving features of the ancient building include some stretches of the walls, the piers and the great arch marking the entrance to the right arm of the transept. The groin vaulting and octagonal structure encasing the dome were built during the Romanesque period to replace the original wooden truss ceiling. The Basilichetta di San Lino, whose original structure dates from the 10th century, stands to the right of the altar.

We now take Via Santa Caterina as far as Largo Richini and then continue along Via Festa del Perdono into the heart or 'hyper-centre' of the city. This street skirts the long side of the **Ca' Granda**, which once housed the Ospedale Maggiore and is now occupied by Milan University. It was

Francesco Sforza that decided in 1456 to build a main hospital for the poor to take the place of the numerous small structures and charitable institutions scattered in different points of the city. The project was entrusted to the Tuscan architect Filarete, who designed a complex in two equal sections, one for men and the other for women, each divided into four square courtyards. The two sections were joined by two more identical courtyards, which were also to accommodate the church. Work began under his personal supervision from the wing nearer San Nazaro. The Lombard masons who took over subsequently introduced some modifications, above all in connection with the façades. A special jubilee known as the *Festa del Perdono* (Feast of Forgiveness) was celebrated every other year to finance this colossal undertaking.

Filarete (Antonio Averlino), Ca' Granda, now occupied by Milan University, cloister

The construction work continued with alternating phases until the beginning of the 19th century. In 1943, after the hospital had been moved to the Niguarda district, the buildings were severely damaged by bombing, with only part of the masonry left standing. Restoration began in 1953 on the basis of plans drawn up by Piero Portaluppi and Liliana Grassi for a whole range of operations including the rebuilding and repair of clearly recognisable parts in their original form, the demolition of severely damaged structures, the removal of additions, and the construction of new, modern facilities for the university, which moved into the Ca' Granda in 1958.

The different sections belonging to the various phases of building can be clearly identified as we walk down Via Festa del Perdono. The first is the 15th-century wing, marked by a portico with stone columns and round arches crowned with a row of double lancet windows and a brick cornice. This is followed by a 17th-century façade of terracotta with a main door providing access to the central courtyard and finally by a neoclassical wing. The Baroque central courtyard is the work of Francesco Maria Ricchino and Fabio Mangone. The façades, which were reassembled by the restorers out of original pieces, are lavishly decorated. The entrance in the middle of the right side of the courtyard provides access to the great space of the intersection that once housed the infirmary, the only part of which left intact is the central structure encasing the dome. A short covered passageway further to the right leads into the earlier and better preserved courtyard, the **Cortile della Spezieria**, surrounded by a two-storey arcade. The adjacent **Cortile dei Bagni** is also a 15th-century construction. An *Annunciation* by Guercino can be seen in the 17th-century Church of the Annunciata, which looks onto the main courtyard.

Continuing northward, we arrive at **Piazza Santo Stefano**, which· once constituted the heart of Milan's retail trade together with the nearby Verziere (historic location of Milan's greengrocery market) and Piazza Fontana. The 17th-century façade of the Church of Santo Stefano, now

deconsecrated and used to house the Diocesan Archives, is situated on the right side of the square. Open to visitors by request, it holds numerous paintings of the Lombard school from the late 16th and early 17th century. The neighbouring **Church of San Bernardino alle Ossa** was founded in medieval times but took its present shape over the period spanning the last few decades of the 17th century and the first half of the 18th century. The 17th-century ossuary chapel to the right of the façade can be entered from inside the church. The very distinctive square chapel has a compositionally daring frescoed ceiling (1695–1698) by Sebastiano Ricci depicting a triumph of souls and glory of angels. The walls are entirely covered in human bones from abolished cemeteries arranged to form patterns and friezes.

Before we set off along Corso di Porta Vittoria, a short detour northward leads us to **Piazza Fontana**. Initially the marketplace for fruit and vegetables, it was redesigned in the 18th century by Giuseppe Piermarini, who also built the fountain to which it owes its name. The branch of the Banca Nazionale dell'Agricoltura on the south side was the scene of a tragic bomb attack on 12 December 1969 that marked the beginning of the years of terrorism. One of the sides of the Arcivescovado or archbishop's see, which stands on the site of the ancient and repeatedly rebuilt **Vescovado** or Bishop's Palace, also looks onto the square. Documented from early medieval times on, the Vescovado was destroyed by the Holy Roman Emperor Frederick I, known as Barbarossa, and then rebuilt. Its completion in 1174 was followed by additions and renova-

5

Guastalla Garden

tions, elements of which survive in the façade on Via Arcivescovado. Pellegrino Tibaldi was commissioned in 1565 to build the imposing courtyard with a rusticated two-storey arcade onto which the quarters of the cathedral's canons open. Piermarini worked on the façade nearest Piazza Fontana in the late 18th century. The apartments of the Arcivescovado are open to visitors by request and hold a rich collection of paintings. The ancient **Palazzo del Capitano di Giustizia** (or Palazzo delle Nuove Carceri) stands nearby in Piazza Beccaria. The building, work on which began in 1578, is arranged around two courtyards and owes the grim appearance evident above all in the first courtyard to its original function as a prison.

We now return to Via del Verziere and turn into Corso di Porta Vittoria. Located on the corner with Via Francesco Sforza is the **Palazzo Sormani Andreani**, one of Milan's most sumptuous 18th-century mansions. Attention should be drawn in particular to the two façades, one on the street with a curved pediment and long balcony, and the other looking onto the garden. The decoration of the interiors was lost as a result of wartime bombing. Some fine canvases by Grechetto, a celebrated master of Genoese Baroque, can be seen in the room named after him. Housed in the building with its hundreds of thousands of books since 1956, the Central Municipal Library also organises exhibitions and conferences.

From the Corso, a short detour along Via della Guastalla will enable us to discover a hidden corner of Milan, namely the **Guastalla Garden** that was once the grounds of the college, founded in the 16th century to ed-

137

Palazzo di Giustizia, designed by Marcello Piacentini, 1932–1940

ucate girls from both noble and poor families. (The entrance is at number 8.) Its age-old trees provide a setting for two pavilions and a delightful 17th-century pond of irregular shape. The **Synagogue** standing opposite the entrance to the small park was designed by Luca Beltrami (1890–1892) and almost entirely destroyed by the bombing of 1943. All that remains of the original building is the oriental-style façade with its facing of stone and polychromatic marble. The interior was rebuilt as a contemporary reinterpretation of the 19th-century design.

We now return to Corso di Porta Vittoria and continue for a short distance until we come on the right to the enormous **Palazzo di Giustizia** (the Court House, 1932–1940) built by Marcello Piacentini in the monumental style typical of the Fascist regime with severe marble façades. Greatly criticised as completely extraneous to the surrounding architectural fabric, the building is trapezoidal in layout and has 1,200 rooms and 65 halls interspersed with large areas of open space. The wealth of original pictorial and sculptural decoration, including works by Carlo Carrà, Achille Funi, Mario Sironi, Arturo Martini, Giacomo Manzù and Fausto Melotti, still survives inside.

Situated in a small square in front of the Palazzo di Giustizia, the **Church of San Pietro in Gessate** was built in the late 15th century with funding from the Florentine banker Pigello Portinari and subjected to large-scale rebuilding designed to restore its original appearance in the 20th century. These operations included building the present façade, which incorporates an earlier entrance. Numerous works of artistic merit are

to be seen in the side chapels of the radically altered interior, including a fresco attributed to Bergognone (fifth chapel on the left) and a cycle of *Episodes from the Life of the Virgin Mary*. Now in a poor state of preservation, the frescoes in the Grifi Chapel in the left transept by the Leonardesque painters Bernardino Butinone and Bernardino Zenale (1490) show *Scenes from the Life of Saint Ambrose* in illusionistic architectural settings.

We now continue along Via Corridoni and then down Via Conservatorio as far as the **Basilica of Santa Maria della Passione** at number 14. It was Daniele Birago, a leading figure in the Sforza court, who decided to build this church in 1485 on a scale second only to the Cathedral. Like so many others in Renaissance Milan, it originally followed Bramante's centrally organised plan, here in the shape of a Greek cross with octagonal base beneath a dome. The external casing of the dome, which can be seen from the outside, was built halfway through the 16th century in the grandiloquent style of Roman mannerism. In compliance with the dictates of the Counter-Reformation, Martino Bassi gave the basilica a longitudinal layout in 1543 with the addition of a three-aisled nave. Completed in the 18th century, the façade is decorated with sculptural works on the theme of the Passion of Christ. Among the works by important 16th- and 17th-century masters to be seen inside, attention should be drawn to the *Deposition* in the right transept, attributed to Bernardino Luini, the *Last Supper* by Gaudenzio Ferrari in the left transept, and the celebrated depiction of *Saint Carlo Borromeo Fasting* by Daniele Crespi. The frescoes in the 15th-century chapter house in the section to the right of the presbytery, which also contains the gallery and the room of furnishings, are by Bergognone. The painter imagined this as a room opening onto an airy loggia occupied by figures from sacred history. The adjoining Old Sacristy is adorned with ten 18th-century wooden panels depicting Biblical scenes.

Leaving the church and turning into Via Bellini, we find one of the masterpieces of Milanese architecture in the Liberty style at number 11, namely **Casa Campanini**, the house that the architect Alfredo Campanini built for himself. He also designed the decoration, from the sculptural figures of the entrance (brilliantly executed in concrete) to the windows and the wrought ironwork with plant motifs. Attention should be drawn to the perfectly preserved hallway, where the various

techniques and materials (iron, fresco, stucco and ceramics) used to create plant-like shapes give birth to an extraordinary unified whole.

Casa Campanini, portal with a female figure

Giuseppe Grandi, Monument to the Five Days, 1881–1895

Located at the end of Corso di Porta Vittoria on the site of the ancient city gate known as the Porta Tosa, the **Piazza Cinque Giornate** was the scene of some important episodes in the resistance to the Austrians during the struggle for national liberation and unification (the Risorgimento). The Monument to the Five Days in the middle of the square commemorating the glorious events of March 1848 is the work of Giuseppe Grandi (1881–1895). The remains of the fallen lie in the crypt beneath its granite base and their names are inscribed on the obelisk, around which realistically modelled and scantily clad female figures personifying the five-day uprising are dynamically arranged. The composition also includes a lion and an eagle, respectively symbolising the brave rebellion of the city of Milan and the oppression of the Austrian empire.

Before continuing outside the city along Corso XXII Marzo, we can walk a short distance down Viale Regina Margherita as far as the **Rotonda della Besana** (Rotunda of Via Besana), the ancient *foppone* (communal grave) of the Ospedale Maggiore. Built in 1713 on the site of the hospital cemetery, the Chapel of San Michele ai Nuovi Sepolcri has the

layout of a Greek cross with an octagonal structure encasing its dome and stands inside an elegant curved portico with semi-circular recesses at regular intervals (1725). After being used for different purposes, it was sold in 1940 to the municipal authorities, who had it restored and turned into a venue for exhibitions surrounded by a public park. Today it houses the **MUBA (Museo dei Bambini)**, a museum offering exhibitions and workshops for children, as well as play areas.

Rotonda della Besana, aerial view

We can now cross the avenue and continue along Via Fogazzaro as far as number 36 and the Prada Foundation exhibition centre, which hosts two projects by contemporary artists of international renown every year. In May 2015 the Foundation inaugurated its new exhibition areas in Largo Isarco, with the citadel of the arts designed by the OMA architecture firm, headed by Rem Koolhas.

From Piazza Medaglie d'Oro, once the site of the ancient gate of Porta Romana at the end of the Corso di Porta Romana, we can also continue outside the city as far as the Abbey of Chiaravalle. The distance (about five kilometres) can be easily travelled by public transport. Founded in 1135 by the abbot of the Cistercian Monastery of Clairvaux in France, the abbey is seen today in the shape it took subsequent to rebuilding in

5

Abbey of Chiaravalle

the 12th century. The complex of the church and connected buildings is richly decorated with frescoes and works by Bernardino Luini, the Campi brothers and the Della Rovere brothers, Giovanni Battista and Giovanni Maura, also known as the Fiammenghini. Importance attaches in architectural terms to the distinctive tower, built on top of the dome to a height of 54 metres in sections marked by lancet windows and arcades, and the partially rebuilt cloister with Gothic arches on small columns and capitals with human and animal shapes.

Returning to Piazza Cinque Giornate, we proceed along Corso XXII Marzo and turn left into Via Cellini to see the 'workers' village' on Via Lincoln, which is screened externally by a sheer wall. It consists of about a 100 two-storey single-family houses with very small gardens looking onto Via Lincoln. This is the only completed part of a huge project for 300 single-family houses and 31 apartment buildings launched in 1886 by the Società Edificatrice di Abitazioni Operaie to turn the area of Porta Vittoria into a sort of workers' town.

We now return to Corso XXII Marzo and proceed on the right as far as **Largo Marinai d'Italia**, an area now occupied by a park but once the site of a vegetable market. The sole survivor of the old market struc-

tures is the **Palazzina Liberty**, a graceful building embellished with floral reliefs and ceramic decorations originally used to serve refreshments.
The scrapping of the Porta Vittoria Railway Station and the creation
of the Dateo-Rogoredo stretch of the new rail link offered an oppor-
tunity to redevelop this area of the city. The block situated adjacent to
Largo Marinai d'Italia between Viale Umbria and Via Cena is to house
a **European Library of Information and Culture** (the BEIC, Biblioteca
Europea di Informazione e Cultura). In addition to the reading rooms
and the various departments and offices, the building will contain conference halls, an educational centre, a media forum, a children's library
with garden and a plaza. The library will also be linked to a multifunctional complex with commercial, residential and public spaces.

Since 2011, the building at Viale Campania 12 has been home to **WOW
Spazio Fumetto**, the museum of comics, illustration and animation set
up and managed by the Franco Fossati Foundation with the aim of con-
serving and promoting Italian and international examples of what has
been described as the 'ninth art'.

From here, continuing for some way along Viale Campania and Viale
Romagna, we reach the Città Studi university complex situated on the
other side of Piazza Leonardo da Vinci. The first sections to be built were
the architecture and engineering faculties of the Milan Polytechnic
(1913–1927). Subsequently, in accordance with a plan of 1913, all of
the scientific faculties were relocated in this area of the city, which is

Monument to
the Unknown Sailor
on Largo Marinai
d'Italia

therefore characterised by the presence of buildings constructed – above all in the first half of the 20th century – to house lecture halls and departments. Attention should be drawn to the schools designed by Luigi Secchi on Piazzale Leonardo, the faculty of architecture at Via Bonardi 3, designed by a team including Gio Ponti, and the open-air swimming pool by Secchi on Via Ampère (95-101). The most recent works include the new Botanical Gardens on Via Golgi and the Museo Zoologico Didattico (Didactic Zoological Museum) on the corner of Via Celoria and Via Golgi.

From Piazza del Duomo to Porta Venezia: The Monumental City between Neoclassical and Deco, and the Bicocca District

6

The itinerary runs through an area studded with stately homes in the northeast of the city, from graceful ancient buildings such as Palazzo Isimbardi and the Villa Reale to a rich variety of modern buildings, above all in the Art Nouveau and Deco styles.

Now completely pedestrianised, the bustling commercial thoroughfare of Corso Vittorio Emanuele II starts from the northeast corner of Piazza del Duomo and follows the course of a Roman road known in the 17th century as the Corsia dei Servi, the name by which it is referred to in Manzoni's novel *I Promessi sposi* (*The Betrothed*). It took its present shape in the 19th century.

Turning immediately left into Via San Paolo, we continue as far as **Piazza del Liberty**, which takes its name from the façade of the building by Giovanni and Lorenzo Muzio (1956–1963) at number 8. This incorporates faux stone elements from the Trianon, a renowned café in the Art Nouveau style known in Italy as Liberty, which once stood on the Corso. Having returned to this main road, we can see on the left, where the road widens, the **Church of San Carlo al Corso**, a solemn neoclassical edifice begun in 1839 and completed in 1847, after the demolition of the Church of Santa Maria dei Servi and the enlargement of the roadway. Preceded by a Corinthian portico and covered with a dome on a tall drum, the building constitutes an original variation on the Pantheon theme.

Corso Vittorio Emanuele leads into **Piazza San Babila**, built on a site once occupied by a complex of five churches. The redevelopment of this area was a key issue in the city's planning scheme of 1927, which ushered in a large-scale construction project including the Palazzo del Toro (1937–1940) with a theatre and commercial gallery on the corner with the Corso. The **Church of San Babila**, one of Milan's most

The former Corso Hotel, detail of the window decoration, 1902–1905 Piazza del Liberty 8

important Romanesque churches, is almost sacrificed in this monumental fabric. Built at the end of the 11th century, it has three aisles ending in semi-circular apses. The octagonal structure on a rectangular base encasing the dome is somewhat later. The church was renovated in the Baroque era with the addition, among other things, of another bay in front and an imposing façade. Large-scale work aimed at restoring the original medieval appearance of the building began at the end of the 19th century. The Neo-Romanesque restoration of the façade was completed at the turn of the century and the 19th-century bell tower was renovated in 1926.

Corso Venezia, a major thoroughfare the first stretch of which once led from the centre to the medieval gate situated in the vicinity of Via del Senato, starts from the piazza. The building at number 10 is **Casa Fontana** (today Casa Silvestri), one of the few private residences of the Renaissance period still to be found in Milan. Long attributed to Bramante, it has undergone repeated renovation. In addition to the fine entrance and terracotta window frames, attention should be drawn to the traces of frescoes with figures and architectural motifs that originally adorned the façade. The building on the opposite side of the road

Collegio Elvetico

is the **Palazzo del Seminario Arcivescovile**, founded by Carlo Borromeo in 1564 and organised around a large internal courtyard built at the beginning of the 17th century with solemn forms in a simple, austere style. The entrance on Corso Venezia, designed by Ricchino, has a caryatid on either side and forms part of an unfinished project of enlargement launched in the first half of the 17th century.

Turning left into Via del Senato a little further along the street, at number 10 we arrive at the **Collegio Elvetico**, built to train Swiss candidates for the priesthood and currently occupied by the State Archives. Designed for Federico Borromeo by Fabio Mangone early in the 17th century, the building is distinguished by formal rigour and clarity endowing it with a solemn and austere appearance. Monumental in style, it is organised around two courtyards with a two-storey colonnade. Ricchino designed the concave façade, some elements of which seem to herald the Baroque.

On returning to Corso Venezia, we arrive almost immediately at the **Palazzo Serbelloni**, one of the most famous and important examples of Milanese neoclassical architecture, on the corner with Via San Damiano. A large recessed loggia with pilasters and columns surmounted by

Palazzo Castiglioni,
sala dei Pavoni
(Peacock Room)
Corso Venezia 47–49

Palazzo Castiglioni,
staircase

a pediment is set in the middle of the façade. The entrance provides access to a colonnaded courtyard and then to the garden through a succession of porticos and vestibules. The richly decorated interiors were largely destroyed during World War II.

Further down on the left side of Corso Venezia (47-49), we find one of the city's most important and significant Art Nouveau buildings, namely the **Palazzo Castiglioni**, the masterpiece of the architect Giuseppe Sommaruga, one of the leading figures in Italian Modernism. Built between 1900 and 1903, it marked the advent of the new century and the new Liberty style in Milanese residential architecture. Crisp and linear in its simple structure, it has an ornate façade of great dynamism and physical exuberance. The decoration by Ernesto Bazzaro displays a whole variety of classical elements and initially included two sculptures of female figures, which were considered too daring and relocated a few days after the inauguration to the inner courtyard of Villa Faccanoni-Romeo (Itinerary 3). The graceful wrought ironwork of

6

the Gothic arches on the ground floor with its gently entwined floral motifs is instead attributed to Alessandro Mazzucotelli. Attention should also be drawn to the façade looking onto the garden as well as the majestic staircase and the Sala dei Pavoni or Peacock Room, with its lavish stucco decoration.

Villa Necchi
Campiglio
Via Mozart 12

Following the Liberty trail, we can continue from Palazzo Castiglioni into the block formed by Via Cappuccini, Via Barozzi and Via Mozart. Particular interest attaches to the **Berri Meregalli Houses**, designed for the Berri Meregalli family by Giulio Ulisse Arata between 1910 and 1914. The one at Via Cappuccini 8 – richly decorated on the outside with carved *putti* and a whole variety of animals including rams, fish, frogs, owls, dogs and lions – is the latest and marks the end of the Liberty style in Milan. The façade of the one at Via Mozart 21 presents frescoes of imposing female figures and decorative elements of a markedly Art Nouveau character. Located in the same area on Via Mozart (11), Via Serbelloni (10-12) and Via Melegari (1-5), the houses designed between 1924 and 1930 by Aldo Andreani are the only completed parts of an organic project to develop the grounds of Palazzo Serbelloni.

At Via Mozart 12 stands the **Villa Necchi Campiglio**, owned by the FAI. Built by Piero Portaluppi (1932–1935), the villa is set in a splendid garden and marks the architect's embrace of the Rationalist approach.

Municipal Museum of Natural History

The perfectly preserved interiors, which he designed down to the smallest details, house two important art collections, namely the De' Micheli, with fine 18th-century French miniatures and paintings of the Venetian school, and the Gian Ferrari, with a group of about forty masterpieces of 20th-century Italian art by painters ranging from Giorgio de Chirico to Mario Sironi.

We now proceed along Via Vivaio as far as the **Palazzo Isimbardi** facing onto Corso Monforte (number 35). Now housing the offices of the Metropolitan City of Milan, it has a grand 18th-century façade with broad stucco cornices and an elegant Renaissance courtyard. Hanging in the Council Room, which is open to visitors on request, is a large canvas by Giovanni Battista Tiepolo from a Venetian palace. The section on the corner with Via Vivaio is a 20th-century addition designed by Giovanni Muzio.

Having returned onto Corso Venezia, we turn left into Via Palestro, which leads to the complex of the Villa Reale and the 19th-century public gardens. The imposing building standing on the corner of the two streets beside the park is the **Civico Museo di Storia Naturale** (Municipal Museum of Natural History). Built by Giovanni Ceruti in the Neo-Romanesque style between 1888 and 1919, it housed one of Europe's most important museums of natural history before bombing in

August 1943 destroyed practically all of the collections on display as well as part of the storerooms and library. The museum, which is also a research centre, is currently one of the most important of its kind in Italy as regards the scale of its collections and the quality of the items exhibited. Attention should be drawn in particular to the dioramas offering faithful reconstructions of the environments and the flora and fauna of parks and nature reserves throughout the world.

Continuing along Via Palestro, we come to the **Boschetti** area on the left corresponding to the present-day Via Marina, a long, straight, tree-lined avenue built by Piermarini as part of the public gardens project. Now transformed by traffic and parked vehicles, it was one of the most frequented spots in the city at the end of the 18th century, as attested among other things in the recollections of Parini and Foscolo. A *Monument to Felice Cavallotti* by Ernesto Bazzaro (1906) stands at the end of this road.

The entrance to Villa Belgiojoso Bonaparte, commonly known as the **Villa Reale** (Royal Palace), is at Via Palestro 16. Ludovico Barbiano di Belgiojoso commissioned Leopoldo Pollack, a pupil of Piermarini, to build the villa in 1790. Its layout of a main courtyard on the street and a richly ornate monumental façade looking onto the garden at the rear is somewhat unusual for Milan. Constituting the truly distinctive element of the villa's architecture, the garden was designed by Ludovico Belgiojoso himself with advice from Pollack as one of the first in Italy to adopt the English style. It takes advantage of the irregular lie of the land to create a varied environment of wooded areas and streams interspersed with faux ruins.

The present furnishings of the villa – which served as a residence for Napoleon and then his viceroy Eugène de Beauharnais and currently

houses the **Gallery of Modern Art** – partially reflect the original neoclassical design.

The Gallery of Modern Art is one of the richest collections in Italy devoted to the art of the 19th century and essential above all to our understanding of painting in the region of Lombardy. Initially housed in the Sforza Castle, it was moved to the Villa Reale in 1921.

Largely the result of generous private bequests, its holdings were reorganised and their display settings redesigned as from 2005. The series of rooms begins with Neoclassicism, and continues through Romanticism to include Realism, the Scapigliatura movement and Divisionism. Among the numerous artists featured, attention should be drawn to Antonio Canova, Francesco Hayez, Tranquillo Cremona, Gaetano Previati, Giovanni Segantini and the sculptor Medardo Rosso. The top floor of the villa houses the **Grassi Collection**, which was donated to the city in 1956. In addition to select works of sculpture, ceramics, ancient carpets and fabrics, this comprises a priceless group of 19th-century French and Italian paintings (Paul Cézanne, Pierre-Auguste Renoir, Vincent Van Gogh, Edouard Manet, Jean-François Millet, Gustave Courbet, Antonio Fontanesi, Giovanni Carnovali known as Piccio and Giovanni Fattori). They are exhibited in Ignazio Gardella's original setting, which constitutes a fine example of post-war Italian museum design. The ground floor of the museum houses the **Vismara Collection**, a substantial group of works by masters such as Raoul

Dufy, Henri Matisse, Georges Rouault and Pablo Picasso as well as 20th-century Italian works, including in particular a significant series of paintings by Giorgio Morandi.

Built by Ignazio Gardella between 1948 and 1954, the **Pavilion of Contemporary Art (PAC)** looks onto a small courtyard of the Villa Reale once occupied by the stables, which were destroyed during the war. The building, one of the most significant works of Italian architecture of the 1950s, was blown up by the Mafia in 1993 and completely destroyed. Subsequently rebuilt by the architect in its original form, it offers a large a flexible space that can be arranged and reorganised according to requirements without losing its original environmental unity. The gallery is divided into three distinct but communicating levels differentiated as volumes flooded with light. The first room looks onto the park through a wall of glass. The second is at a higher level and receives light from above through a skylight. The third is an elevated rectangular structure with artificial lighting and a balcony looking onto the second. It is used exclusively for exhibitions focusing on the most recent and multiform developments in contemporary art.

The area in front of the Villa Reale is occupied by the **Gardens of Porta Venezia**, the first public park to be created in Europe (1783). Land made available by the suppression of two monasteries was shaped by the architect Piermarini into an Italian-style garden with a predictable layout well suited to public use. The Austrian emperor Franz Josef I

6

Pavilion of
Contemporary Art,
view of the interior

Giovanni Battista
Tiepolo, *Allegory*,
1731
Palazzo Dugnani

had the park enlarged in 1857 by Giuseppe Balzaretto, the creator together with Emilio Alemagna (1881) of a romantic setting with the in-
troduction of fountains, waterfalls, hills and faux rock effects. In accordance with Piermarini's original design, the park ends with a flight
of steps connecting it with the bastions of Porta Venezia, which mark
its northern boundary. Among other things, it contains a **Planetarium**
donated to the city by the publisher Ulrico Hoepli and located adjacent to the natural history museum. Designed by the architect Piero
Portaluppi (1930) along classical lines based on the Pantheon, the build-

ing hosts conferences and film shows of a popularising character. The entire inner surface of the dome constitutes the screen onto which images of the starry sky and astronomical phenomena are projected. The profile of the carved panels at the base of the dome reproduces the shapes of the buildings on the Milanese horizon as seen from the gardens of Porta Venezia in the 1930s.

The **Palazzo Dugnani**, one of the numerous aristocratic mansions characterising this area of the city, is located at Via Manin 2 on the edge of the park. Built in the late 17th century and renovated in the second half of the 18th century, it was restored after the bombing of World War II. Stretching two storeys in height and fitted with a wrought iron balcony, the main hall still has a huge allegorical fresco by Giovanni Battista Tiepolo (1731) on the ceiling as well as medallions on the walls depicting the *Exploits of Scipio and Masinissa* by the same hand.

6

Together with the arches of Porta Ticinese, the **Arches of Porta Nuova** standing in the nearby Piazza Cavour constitute the sole survivors of the medieval city walls. The ancient gate consisted of two arched passageways flanked by towers, which were knocked down in the period of Spanish rule when the new ring of walls made the ancient fortifications obsolete and they were incorporated into private buildings. In 1861, against the background of renewed interest in the monuments of medieval Milan, the gate was restored and freed from the structures built up around it in the meantime. Two pedestrian passageways were opened in the towers and the main structure was decorated with the addition of fine artefacts from the Roman era, now replaced with copies. The

Giovanni Battista Tiepolo, *The Generosity of Scipio*, 1731 Palazzo Dugnani

161

marble tabernacle on the external façade dates from the time of the Visconti dynasty.

We now leave the square by way of Via Turati and turn down Via Carlo Porta. The house at number 5 is known as the Casa delle Rondini because of the polychromatic majolica decoration of swallows by Ernesto Treccani covering the entire façade. Since 1978 it has housed the **Corrente Foundation**, created by Treccani himself and a group of like-minded artists and intellectuals to promote the study of the historical period between the birth of the Corrente movement – founded by the artist in 1938 – and Realism. **Treccani's Studio**, which is open to the public, presents a collection of paintings, drawings, sculpture and ceramics that document the entire course of his artistic trajectory. Further along, at the intersection of Via Turati and Via Moscova, we find on the right a building composed of two parts separated by a private road and occupying an entire block. The building, completed in 1922, was at once derisively dubbed **Ca' Brutta** – the 'ugly house' – to indicate distaste for the innovative vocabulary adopted by the architect Giovanni Muzio. The city's first sensational example of Art Deco, the building combines materials of different colours in a sophisticated ensemble of architectural elements from the classical tradition.

The building at number 34 on the right is the home of the Società per le Belle Arti ed Esposizione Permanente, founded in 1833 to promote painting and sculpture. Known as the **Palazzo della Permanente** and

162

Customs house at
Porta Venezia

6

used to host exhibitions, it was built by Luca Beltrami with a façade in the Tuscan Renaissance style and restructured internally by Achille and Piergiacomo Castiglioni, who also designed the tower at the rear. Via Turati leads into **Piazza della Repubblica**, which stands on the site occupied by Milan's first railway station in the 19th century and was the fulcrum in the 1930s of a huge project that transformed the layout of the entire northern section of the city. The area stretching west of Piazza della Repubblica toward Porta Nuova and Porta Garibaldi (see Itinerary 8) has been the scene of a complex redevelopment project. Among other things, this has led to the creation of gardens at Porta Nuova and of an innovative and original 'Biblioteca degli Alberi' (Library of Trees) providing information about plants and flowers along its pathways and a Museum of Flowers and Insects; some areas will be occupied by ponds and others paved over to provide adequate spaces for various activities. Buildings and pavilions located inside the park and on its edges will house a fashion school, museum and exhibition centre.

Proceeding northward from the piazza, we can turn right before arriving at the Central Railway Station and visit the bastions of Porta Venezia, which were redeveloped in the 18th century as a splendid tree-lined promenade for pedestrians and carriages after losing their defensive function. Today they are a main artery for the city's traffic.

The road ends with Piazza Oberdan on the site of the old **Porta Venezia**, one of the eight main gates in the Spanish walls, which were converted

in the neoclassical period to serve as customs barriers and triumphal entrances into the city. The two tollgates (1827–1828) that separate Corso Venezia from Corso Buenos Aires were built for this purpose by Rodolfo Vantini and decorated with sculptures by the best-known artists of the time. The bas-reliefs in the upper corners of the façades depict episodes in Milan's history. In the square, Spazio Oberdan houses the **Cineteca di Milano**. This film library, established in 1947, conserves and promotes cinematographic culture both in Italy and abroad. It screens over 400 films a year and also organises talks, performances and various other events, including the festival 'Italian Cinema as Seen from Milan'. In 2014, the **MIC (Interactive Museum of Cinema)** was set up along Viale Zara, which may be reached by travelling on metro line M5. The museum screens films, sequences and animated features from the archives of the Cineteca.

The **Casa Torre Rasini** (Rasini Tower House, 1933–1936) on the corner with Corso Venezia is the work of the architects Lancia and Ponti. While the marble-covered building is Rationalist in style, the tower is still strongly influenced by the Novecento movement.

From the piazza, before taking Corso Buenos Aires, we can make a short detour into Via Malpighi, where the **Galimberti** and **Guazzoni Houses** at numbers 3 and 12, both the work of the architect Giovan Battista Bossi, provide two different interpretations of the Liberty style.

Casa Galimberti,
detail of the
ceramic decoration
of the façade
Via Malpighi 3

Boschi-Di Stefano
House Museum,
view of one of
the rooms

6

Built between 1902 and 1905, the Casa Galimberti is characterised by its exuberant painted ceramic decoration. Gigantic polychromatic figures, mostly female, and luxuriant plant motifs cover the façades almost entirely and emphasise their vertical development. The Casa Guazzoni is instead distinguished by decorations of wrought iron and concrete. The arches on the ground floor are interspersed with expressive female heads (all of which are different) and a graceful floral frieze runs around the middle of the first floor. After a stretch of Corso Buenos Aires, the itinerary takes us into Viale Tunisia and the Via Jan, where the **Boschi-Di Stefano House Museum** can be visited at number 15.

Located inside an Art Deco building designed by the architect Portaluppi, it was inaugurated in 2003 and hosts an important collection of about 2,000 works of 20th-century Italian art donated to the city in 1973, including canvases by Filippo de Pisis, Carlo Carrà, Lucio Fontana, Giorgio de Chirico, Giorgio Morandi and Mario Sironi.

Viale Tunisia ends at a junction with Via Vittor Pisani, which leads directly to the **Stazione Centrale** (Central Railway Station).

Inaugurated in 1931 and facing onto Piazza Duca d'Aosta, the station constitutes a sort of ideal link between the Liberty period and the subsequent development of Art Deco. Monumentally designed by Ulisse Stacchini in 1912 on a colossal scale with architectural structure and decoration constituting an inseparable whole, it displays a curious mixture of references to German culture, explicitly Art Deco formulas, and details that seem to herald Modernism.

Among the numerous works of sculpture animating the complex, attention should be drawn in particular to the two winged horses crown-

On this page and opposite Central Railway Station, façade and detail showing *Progress Led by Will*

6

ing the façade, the medallions by the platforms, and the statues and medallions by the ticket-offices as well as the ceramic panels with views of the city in the concourse. The most exquisitely Art Deco sections are those of the royal pavilion facing platform 21, where stone facing, sculptural elements and mosaic panels combine with the furnishings in a graceful small-scale variation on the palatial theme.

Along the embankment on Via Ferrante Aporti a **Holocaust Memorial** was inaugurated in 2013: a museum area established as a place of remembrance, as well as of dialogue between different religions, ethnicities and cultures. From the so-called platform 21, hundreds of Jews and political prisoners steeped in cattle cars were deported to the camps of Auschwitz-Birkenau, Mauthausen, Bergen Belsen, Fossoli and Bolzano. Designed by Ponti, Nervi and Danusso and built between 1955 and 1960, the **Pirelli Skyscraper** stands on the left side of Piazza Duca d'Aosta. The '**Pirellone**', as it is commonly known, currently houses the offices of Lombardy's regional government and constitutes an exceptional example of structural and technological optimisation combined with what is an unusual image for a tower block. Ponti's design and the tapered sides of the façades endow the building with a sort of graceful, dynamic lightness accentuated by the fact that it changes in appearance when seen from different viewpoints. Among other things, the restoration work completed in 2005 has made it possible to regain use of the more important sections and to convert some areas for institutional and official functions.

From Piazza Duca d'Aosta it is possible to reach in roughly half an hour by metro the Bicocca district, a vast area situated northeast of

169

Palazzo Lombardia

The international call for tenders for the designing of the new offices of the Lombardy regional government was won by the American firm Pei, Cobb, Freed & Partners together with the Italian studio Caputo Partnership. The team leader was the well-known Chinese-American architect Ieoh Ming Pei who, among other things, designed the famous Louvre pyramid. The internationally acclaimed architect has chosen to emphasise the strategic position of the new complex within the city. The 161-metre-tall skyscraper, a fully glass-encased reinforced structure, is set on a 'basement' formed by four buildings which, like adjacent sinuous strands, make it accessible from different sides. These passages create an access to a central, oval-shaped, covered central plaza, envisaged as the heart of the project, as well as part of the city. The defining feature of this group of lower buildings is that they converge in certain areas, creating intersections in which the vertical connections are located, along with some of the routes linking the various sections of the complex. Rising from one of these points of contact between the four strands is the towering body of the skyscraper, which houses the Presidential and Management offices. All in all, the complex consists of three elements: an articulated base, a vertical tower-shaped body and a geometrically designed garden. In 2012, the prestigious Council on Tall Buildings and Urban Habitat (CTBUH) of Chicago awarded Palazzo Lombardia as Europe's best skyscraper in terms of design, sustainability and innovation – it was the first Italian building to receive this acknowledgement.

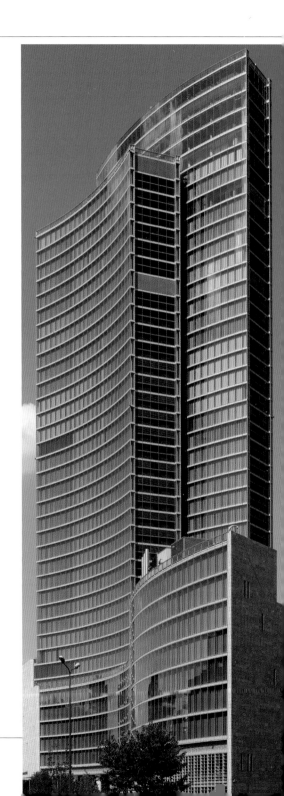

171

The headquarters
of the Università
degli Studi della
Bicocca

Pirelli Headquarters

the city around the main axis of Viale Sarca. This was once the location of the Pirelli chemical plants, but the gradual decrease in production and the partial replacement of industry with services paved the way for a massive project of urban redevelopment launched by the company itself and based on plans drawn up by the architect Vittorio Gregotti. Involving an area of 960,000 square metres, this is the largest operation of urban transformation ever carried out in Italy and second at the European level only to Berlin. The district is designed to serve as a multifunctional area for housing, offices, industry, shopping centres and university departments, combining elements of industrial archaeology and new buildings with a high level of technological innovation.

The building on the corner of Viale Sarca and Viale Pirelli that houses the Pirelli Headquarters can be taken as a symbol of this philosophy. Designed by Gregotti, it is a massive cube incorporating the old cooling tower in a great hall with a glass front. The façade looks onto the **Bicocca degli Arcimboldi**, a suburban villa dating from the Renaissance but largely restored in the 20th century, with interesting sgraf-

Anselm Kiefer,
*Seven Heavenly
Palaces*, 2004
Hangar Bicocca

fito work, frescoes and terracotta decorations on the outside. The building, which is not open to the public, holds a priceless cycle of paintings on courtly themes.

The **Hangar Bicocca** in Via Chiese was a huge factory producing coils for electric train engines. The inside has been painted dark blue all over and the outside clad in a shell of silver-coloured metal.

This space of great visual impact and overtones of science fiction houses a centre with a markedly experimental approach that organises exhibitions, studies and training in the field of contemporary art.

With a view to the direct involvement of artists in a dynamic dialogue of spectators and creators, the Hangar Bicocca supports the development of site-specific projects such as Anselm Kiefer's *Seven Heavenly Palaces*, presented at the inauguration in 2004 and now a permanent installation. The seven monumental towers of lead and reinforced concrete – which look as though they have been forgotten by history and ravaged by time and human neglect – draw inspiration from the cabala and symbolise the mystic experience of ascent through the seven levels of spirituality.

The other important buildings in the Bicocca district include the two university complexes (for sciences and humanities), the headquarters

174

6

Theatre of
the Arcimboldi

of the Deutsche Bank (by Gino Valle), and the **Theatre of the Arcimboldi**. Designed by Gregotti, this is a sober and sophisticated whole made up of three units clad in light-coloured plaster, namely the theatre, the foyer and the fly tower receiving light from a sloping wall of glass. As regards the residential buildings, the Esplanade is a highly complex structure including some green areas.

From Piazza del Duomo to Porta Garibaldi:
The Districts of Museums, Artists and Fashion

7

Running through a vast section in the north of the city, this itinerary takes in two of Milan's best-known areas, namely the Fashion district, with its smart buildings and luxury shops designed by today's top architects, and Brera, with its galleries and the clubs and cafés frequented by students of the academy. This is, however, also an area with a wealth of museums, first and foremost the Pinacoteca di Brera but without forgetting some municipal institutions of an essentially historical nature and the Bagatti Valsecchi and Poldi Pezzoli House Museums.

The monumental arch of the **Galleria Vittorio Emanuele II** is set into the Palazzo dei Portici Settentrionali on the left side of Piazza del Duomo. Forming part of Giuseppe Mengoni's overall plan of redevelopment for the square, the gallery is one of the most important architectural works completed in Milan subsequent to Italy's unification. The idea was prompted by the need to create a link between Piazza del Duomo and the thoroughfare leading to the railway station, which was then located in Piazza della Repubblica. It was decided to opt for a covered gallery made up of two arcades meeting at right angles in an octagonal central plaza known as the Octagon. The plans drawn up by Mengoni, who fell to his death from the scaffolding, were characterised by large-scale adoption of iron and glass for the roofs, the most innovative step imaginable at the time, and the huge proportions of the project, the main arcade being 196 metres in length and the dome over the octagonal plaza 39 metres in diameter. Equally characteristic – and often bitterly criticised – was the lavish decoration. The roofs and floors were rebuilt after the destruction caused by bombing in 1943 and **Camparino**, situated immediately to the left of the entrance, is the sole survivor of the cafés originally opened in the gallery.

Galleria Vittorio
Emanuele II,
the Octagon

Following pages
Teatro alla Scala

177

Gallerie d'Italia
di Piazza Scala

In 2011, a new museum was inaugurated in the Palace of the Banca Commerciale Italiana: the Gallerie d'Italia di Piazza Scala, established in order to display the rich collection owned by Intesa Sanpaolo. The works of art are at the moment divided according to two chronological subdivisions. The 19th-century section of the museum is located in Palazzo Anguissola Antona Traversi; the 20th-century one in the historic headquarters of the Banca Commerciale in Piazza della Scala. Through an itinerary extending from Antonio Canova to Umberto Boccioni, the

Fondazione Cariplo and Intesa Sanpaolo collections span an entire century of art history: the Italian 19th century. The display opens with a magnificent series of thirteen bas-reliefs sculpted by Canova in the late 18th-century and ends with a highly symbolic transition to the 20th-century: the four masterpieces from Boccioni's pre-Futurist season. As a whole, the guiding thread of the Cantiere del '900 section traces a path across Italian art from the 1950s to the 1990s. It highlights the different currents of Abstraction, Art Informel, and formal and technological experimentation, along with the new possibilities that emerged in terms of self-expression and the representation of contemporary man and society.

Antonio Canova,
The Dance of the Sons of Alcinous,
detail, 1790–1792

Umberto Boccioni,
Factories at Porta Romana, detail,
1909–1910

The main arcade runs into **Piazza della Scala**. Built in 1858 on the site of a highly built-up area, the square owes its appearance to the work of Luca Beltrami, who first designed the rear façade of Palazzo Marino and then the two buildings of the Banca Commerciale Italiana, one of which is today occupied by municipal offices. This created the monumental setting for the façade of La Scala, which originally looked onto a fairly narrow street. In accordance with its mission to promote and popularise contemporary art, the activities of the **Nicola Trussardi Foundation** at number 5 include holding two events a year in public spaces in historical, monumental or forgotten parts of the city.

Milan's reputation in the world of music was already solidly established when Giuseppe Piermarini began the construction of La Scala in 1776. The new opera house – the previous one had been an annex of what is now the Palazzo Reale – was called the **Teatro alla Scala** because it was built on the site of the 14th-century Church of Santa Maria della Scala, which took its name in turn from Beatrice Regina della Scala, its founder and the wife of Bernabò Visconti. Subjected to extension and renovation during the 19th century, the building was destroyed by bombing and rebuilt in its original form immediately after the war. The decoration of the horseshoe-shaped interior with its stalls arranged in four tiers of boxes and *loggione* of two galleries dates from the 19th century. La Scala was subjected over the period 2001–2004 to a complex and in fact rather controversial operation of restoration and renovation under the guidance of the architect Mario Botta. In addition to improving the structures and restoring the boxes and stalls, Botta's project involved rebuilding the stage, which can now accommodate three different scenes at the same time. An oval building of stone was added at the rear to house the dressing rooms and the fly tower above the stage was rebuilt on a larger scale than before. The two new sections, which are clearly visible from the square behind Piermarini's solemn façade, are markedly contemporary in appearance.

The building also includes a museum (the **Museo Teatrale alla Scala**, refurbished in 2004) of artistic objects and items connected with La Scala and its historical associations with figures such as Toscanini, Verdi and Rossini. One room is devoted to the display of select items from the splendid collection of sketches created for its productions. A number of short walks lead from the piazza to some places of historical and artistic interest in the maze of streets that characterises this part of Milan's ancient urban fabric. Located at Via Clerici 5, the **Palazzo Clerici** was built in the 18th century on the site of an existing edifice by the marquis Giorgio Antonio Clerici, a Spanish grandee and

7

183

ambassador, who accommodated the archducal family there from 1773 to 1778. The central section of the asymmetric façade is recessed with respect to the street. The courtyard has an arcade of twin columns on only two sides, namely the one including the entrance and the one opposite, which provides access to the smaller second courtyard. The three ramps of the main staircase decorated with anthropomorphic figures of stone begin to the right. The fresco on the ceiling is attributed to Giovanni Battista Piazzetta. The sumptuous furnishings, the quality of the stucco mouldings and the presence of numerous works of art on the first floor bear witness to the prestige of the Clerici family. Adorned with mirrors and drapes, the Gallery of Tapestries has a great frescoed ceiling by Giovanni Battista Tiepolo (circa 1740) depicting the *Chariot of the Sun* with human and mythological figures and animals in an extraordinary combination of luminous transparency and compositional daring.

Via Marino leads from Piazza della Scala into the small Piazza San Fedele with the **Church of San Fedele** and the Palazzo Marino. The church belonged to the Order of Jesuits and is one of the best examples of Counter-Reformation religious architecture. Its construction began in 1569 and involved three of the greatest Milanese architects of the time, namely Pellegrino Tibaldi, Martino Bassi and Francesco Maria Ricchino, one after the other. Distinguished by their inlaid decoration of urban views and landscapes with details in mother-of-pearl, the 16th-century wooden choir stalls from Santa Maria della Scala have been reassembled in the apse. Left unfinished in 1568 after ten years of work, the **Palazzo Marino** was confiscated from its owner, a Genoese financier, and partially completed in the 17th century. It is now municipal property and used as the main headquarters of the Milan city council. Like the sides looking onto the splendid main courtyard, the three-storey façade displays the abundance of sculptural decoration characteristic of Galeazzo Alessi, the architect commissioned by Tommaso Marino. The original plans also envisaged the construction of a street to be lined with other stately mansions linking the building and the cathedral square. The model for this in both formal and financial terms was the Strada Nuova in Genoa, on which Alessi constructed a large number of buildings. The **Church of San Raffaele**

7

Church of San Fedele

185

stands in the nearby Via San Raffaele. Rebuilt after 1575 by Carlo Borromeo, the church has an unusual façade in that the lower section presents an array of gigantic male heads in stone. Some important works by leading Milanese painters of the early 17th century can be seen inside.

Via Case Rotte leads from Piazzetta San Fedele and into Via degli Omenoni, which takes its name from the **Casa degli Omenoni**, a typical example of an artist's house probably built between 1562 and 1566 by the sculptor Leone Leoni. The curious name derives from the presence on the façade of eight telamones, stone columns carved in the shape of male figures that divide the lower storey into bays and support the semi-columns of the upper level. The Michelangelesque vigour of this design made the house a point of reference for Milanese architecture. The building is organised around a rectangular courtyard that is colonnaded on three sides and opens into the garden. The lower storey presents an array of Doric columns with horizontal lintels. The walls of the first floor are divided by Ionic pilasters alternately framing windows with open-topped pediments and niches with unbroken cornices, recently converted into windows.

This small street leads into a small square dominated by the **Palazzo Belgiojoso**, which Prince Alberico XII Barbiano di Belgiojoso commissioned Giuseppe Piermarini to build in 1772. The imposing façade with its wealth of architectural and decorative detail is distinguished by the use of rustication on the lower storey and a giant order of semi-columns and composite pilasters to frame the main entrance. The bays between the columns are occupied by parapets and balustrades, win-

House of
Alessandro
Manzoni

7

dows with projecting cornices and panels with bas-reliefs of heraldic devices and symbolic subjects. The interior develops around a main courtyard and two smaller ones at the sides. It is divided into private homes and not open to the public. The structure, decoration and fittings display an extraordinary degree of stylistic unity deriving from Piermarini's design. Located on the short side of Piazzetta Belgioioso on the corner with Via Morone is the **House of Alessandro Manzoni**, who died there in 1873. The author's library and all the editions of his writings are held in the National Centre of Manzonian Studies and his studio can be visited among other things in the Manzonian Museum, both of which are housed in the building.

Piazza della Scala also marks the beginning of Via Manzoni, which follows the course of the ancient road that led to the Porta Nuova of the Roman era – at the crossroads with Via Borgonuovo and Via Monte Napoleone – and to the medieval gate of the same name. The important buildings on the street include two in the neoclassical style at numbers 6 and 10, both designed by Luigi Cagnola.

Immediately adjacent is the **Poldi Pezzoli Museum**, founded as the private museum of the collector Giangiacomo Poldi Pezzoli and opened to the public in accordance with his wishes in 1881, shortly after his death. It occupies one of the two family mansions, the other being next door at number 14. A keen collector of works in gold, silver, enamel, glass and jewellery, fabrics, furniture, sculptures, ancient books and weapons, archaeological artefacts and paintings, Poldi Pezzoli had the mansion restructured to house his precious collections by Giuseppe Balzaretto over the period 1850–1853. The re-

Poldi Pezzoli
Museum, room
of weapons,
designed by
Arnaldo Pomodoro

Sandro Botticelli,
*Lamentation over
the Dead Christ*,
1495–1500
Poldi Pezzoli
Museum

Piero del Pollaiolo,
Portrait of a Lady,
circa 1470
Poldi Pezzoli
Museum

sult was an eclectic and highly ornate setting in which the works and
furnishings came to form a harmoniously unified whole. While the
rooms were unfortunately subjected to severe damage during World
War II, restoration has proved at least partially successful in some
cases, one of these being the Byzantine Study, which was the collector's
private study and holds examples of medieval, Moorish, Celtic and
Pre-Raphaelite art.

It would be hard to list all the important items of the collection, which
followed the normal practice of the time and ignored any narrow focusing of interest in its search for masterpieces regardless of all criteria
of period, origin and technique. A Persian hunting carpet (1542–1543)
thus rubs shoulders with paintings by Lucas Cranach the Elder, a tea
and coffee set of Meissen china with an 18th-century aspergillum in
coral and enamel. The collector's tastes were more sharply defined in
the field of painting, with a marked interest in 14th and 15th-centu-
ry Italian works, from Tuscany in particular, as well as the school of
Leonardo da Vinci and 18th-century Venetian art. Andrea Mantegna,
Piero della Francesca, Sandro Botticelli and Giovanni Bellini are among
the most important painters whose works are exhibited. The museum
also includes a room displaying the Collection of Clocks donated by
Bruno Falck (the most important one of its kind on public view in Italy)
and a fascinating room of weapons designed by Arnaldo Pomodoro.

We now turn right from Via Manzoni into Via Monte Napoleone,
which follows the line of the Roman city walls and takes its name from
a 19th-century bank. Almost completely altered in appearance dur-

ing the neoclassical period, as were the neighbouring streets, it is lined with a number of aristocratic mansions, including the **Palazzo Melzi di Cusano** at number 18 and **Palazzo Gavazzi**, which houses the **Mario Buccellati Company Museum**, at number 23. Among other things, the items exhibited in the museum include some period pieces by Mario Buccellati, jeweller to Gabriele D'Annunzio.

Turning left off Via Monte Napoleone into Via Santo Spirito, we find the two **Bagatti Valsecchi Mansions** standing opposite one another at numbers 7 and 10. Designed by their original owners, the brothers Fausto and Giuseppe Bagatti Valsecchi, they are both marked by a programmatic return to the architectural vocabulary of the Renaissance. While the influence of Bramante can be seen in the one at number 7, inaugurated in 1895, and the other (1878–1883) is more Lombard in character, they are in any case characterised by the inclusion of ancient architectural fragments of varying origin or copies of 15th and 16th-century elements. The interiors were designed to house the works of art lovingly collected by the two brothers, which can now be seen in the **Bagatti Valsecchi House Museum** (entrance at Via Gesù 5, opened to the public in 1994). Decorated after the model of the ducal palaces in Mantua and Urbino, the apartments display Renaissance furnishings, ceilings, friezes and paintings as well as tapestries, ceramics, musical instruments and ancient weapons.

With its sober exterior and sophisticated interiors, the **Palazzo Morando Attendolo Bolognini** at Via Sant'Andrea 6 is a typical example of aristocratic Milanese architecture of the 18th century. The building was donated to the city in 1945 and is now one of the two seats of the historical collections of the City of Milan.

The museum, known as **Palazzo Morando – Costume, Moda, Immagine**, occupies the first floor of the building and is divided into two parts, namely the picture gallery and the monumental apartment. Attention should be drawn in particular to the paintings that show the ancient face of the city, often bearing witness to the now lost appearance of buildings and places, and thus provide iconographic documentation of changes in the urban fabric and aspects of public and private life in Milan between the 17th and 19th century. Chinese and Japanese porcelain from the Morando family collection can be seen in the richly decorated monumental apartment together with a number of paintings. In 2010 the displays in Palazzo Morando were refurbished, lending new visibility to its remarkable civic art collection. The work carried out has enhanced not just the textiles but also the clothes, accessories and uniforms of the historical collections.

Before continuing along Via Borgonuovo in the direction of Brera, we can return to the last stretch of Via Manzoni and the 18th-century **Church of San Francesco di Paola** with its dynamic façade of

A room of the Palazzo Morando – Costume, Moda, Immagine Museum

concave and convex sections. Sumptuous altars of bronze and precious marble, Rococo confessionals and elegant wooden choir stalls can be seen inside. The building at number 30 (**Palazzo Gallarati Scotti**, formerly Palazzo Spinola) contains a fresco attributed to Tiepolo and a group of canvases by Alessandro Magnasco (1691). Located on the other side at number 41 is the **Palazzo Borromeo d'Adda**, built by the marquis Febo d'Adda around 1820 and substantially altered over the following decades. It is rather austere in appearance. The very wide façade is divided into three horizontal sections, the one corresponding to the first floor showing the only signs of animation in its alternation of triangular and arched pediments. The building is organised around three courtyards aligned parallel to the street. A sumptuous staircase leads up to the family apartment, which was a meeting place for artists and writers in the 19th century and still retains some neoclassical and romantic decorations in a pseudo-Moorish style.

Walking back from Via Manzoni along Via Borgonuovo, an aristocratic street with roots in the 18th century, we find more neoclassical mansions of note at numbers 11 and 23, respectively **Palazzo Orsini** and **Palazzo Moriggia**. The latter is a sober and dignified edifice typical of Giuseppe Piermarini's architectural style and now houses the **Museum of the Risorgimento**. Constituting the nucleus of the city's historical collections together with the Municipal Museum of Milan and the Municipal Museum of Contemporary History, the museum holds works and items ranging from the Napoleonic period to the incorporation of Rome into the Kingdom of Italy (1796–1870). The rooms exhibit printed documents, paintings, weapons and objects once owned by figures such as Napoleon, Garibaldi and Mazzini. Some of the works are by skilled painters such as Gerolamo Induno and of interest in not only historical but also artistic terms. The building alongside is the **Palazzo Landriani**, which has a 16th-century façade and courtyard and a fine 17th-century staircase.

We now proceed along Via Fiori Oscuri to the **Palazzo di Brera**, originally a Jesuit college but now housing a number of cultural institutions. It was built in an area known as the Braida del Guercio, from which the name Brera derives, on the site of an old monastery of the Humiliati order. As the structure proved unable to cope with the great influx of students, it was decided that radical alterations should be made. The project was initially entrusted to Martino Bassi and then to Francesco Maria Ricchino, whose plans were drawn up in 1615 but not put into effect until 1651. Concealed behind the uncompromising block-like exterior of brick is a large central courtyard with

arcades on two storeys connected by the two flights of a monumental staircase. The few decorative elements, limited to the window frames and the rusticated quoins, do little to alter the overall air of sobriety. Giuseppe Piermarini built the majestic entrance in the second half of the 18th century. The bronze monument to Napoleon, depicted as Mars the Bringer of Peace, was cast in 1811 to designs by Antonio Canova and moved to its present position in the middle of the courtyard in 1859.

While the suppression of the Society of Jesus in 1772 led to new governmental and secular functions for the Palazzo di Brera, some of the Jesuits' institutions continued to operate there, especially the school and the library. A library founded by Maria Theresa of Austria was moved into the building in 1773 and subsequently combined with the Jesuit Library to constitute the original nucleus of the present **Biblioteca Nazionale** (National Library), which is still housed there. The **Academy of Fine Arts** then founded by the Empress in 1776 has also been housed in the building ever since and now operates as a public university for art and music. Also located in the Palazzo di Brera is an **Astronomical Observatory** set up by two Jesuits (1760–1765) and currently involved in research in the most important sectors of modern astronomy. The adjoining **Botanical Gardens** were founded by Maria Theresa in 1774 and have recently been restored.

The **Pinacoteca di Brera**, one of Italy's most important collections of paintings, was founded in 1803 as a complement to the academy and originally focused essentially on works of little intrinsic value regarded as suitable for copying by the students as models. Its holdings soon expanded exponentially with the influx of works from the churches and monasteries of religious bodies suppressed not only in Lombardy but also in other territories belonging to the Italian Kingdom, the capital of which was Milan. It is to this situation that the collection owes its specific character, differing from others formed in the same period and the same way by the fact of not being confined to an exclusively local sphere. The museum was officially inaugurated in 1809 but did not become totally independent of the academy until 1882. While the last overall project of reorganisation and renovation was carried out by Vittorio Gregotti over the period 1984–1991, further changes in layout have since been introduced. Launched in 1976, the 'Grande Brera' project has yet to be put into effect and thus retains all its vital relevance. The initial idea was to expand and modernise the museum with the incorporation of the nearby Palazzo Citterio, but the plans drawn up in 1986 by James Stirling have been shelved. It now appears that the

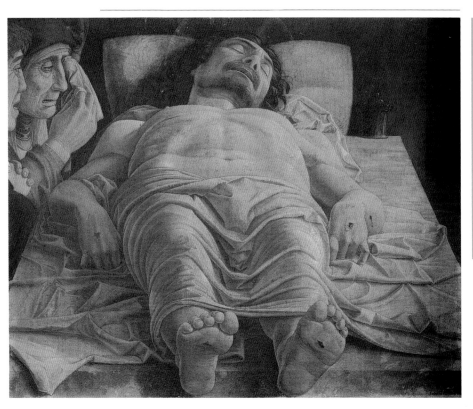

Andrea Mantegna,
*Lamentation over
the Dead Christ*,
circa 1500
Pinacoteca di Brera

relocation of part of the Academy will make new spaces available for the collection.

The Pinacoteca is so extraordinarily well endowed with masterpieces that it would be difficult to list them all. They are laid out in chronological order beginning with the works with gilded backgrounds and Gothic paintings of courtly scenes, including the outstanding *Polyptych of Valle Romita* by Gentile da Fabriano. Great importance attaches to the section of 15th and 16th-century masters from the Veneto region, with renowned works by Andrea Mantegna, Giovanni Bellini, Titian and Tintoretto. The school of Ferrara is also well represented with works by Cosmè Tura, Francesco del Cossa and Ercole de' Roberti as well as Carlo Crivelli from the Marche region. Room XXIV presents works by artists linked in various ways with Urbino, including three of the best-known masterpieces of the entire collection: Bramante's *Christ at the Column*, Raphael's *Marriage of the Virgin* and Piero della Francesca's *Brera Altarpiece*. A great deal of space is also devoted to the 17th and 18th centuries, the latter with a particular focus on Venice (Giovanni Battista Tiepolo, Giovanni Battista Piazzetta, Canaletto and

The *Brera Altarpiece* by Piero della Francesca

The altarpiece painted by Piero della Francesca for the Mausoleum of Federico da Montefeltro, duke of Urbino, is a work of supreme artistic quality and great impact despite its moderate size.

It is a traditional work in terms of iconography with the Madonna and Child enthroned in the centre and surrounded by saints and angels with the kneeling figure of Federico, the donor, in armour in the foreground. According to some historians, the work was commissioned in 1472, the year in which Federico celebrated the birth of his son Guidobaldo and the taking of Volterra, which would account for his decision to be portrayed in military attire. The year was also marked by the death of his beloved wife Battista Sforza, whose name and memory seem to be suggested in the painting by the presence of John the Baptist, San Giovanni Battista in Italian, facing the donor in the very position that she would have occupied. The depiction of Mary keeping tender watch over the slumbering Jesus can also be seen as a delicate allusion to Battista's death in childbirth.

In religious terms, the altarpiece is a solemn meditation on the Marian dogma. The Virgin watching over the body of Christ is in fact identified with the Church as guardian of the Eucharist, and this analogy also gives deeper meaning to the painter's emphasis on the architecture of the churchly building in which the scene is set. At the same time, the celebrated ostrich egg hanging over the head of the Virgin, an object of almost hypnotic attraction, is to be read as a symbol of the Immaculate Conception. It was in fact believed in ancient times that ostrich eggs were fertilised by the sun's rays, hence the analogy with conception through the agency of the Holy Spirit and the virgin birth.

Piero della Francesca, *Brera Altarpiece*, circa 1472 Pinacoteca di Brera

7

Caravaggio
(Michelangelo
Merisi), *Supper at
Emmaus*, 1606
Pinacoteca di Brera

Raphael, *The
Marriage of the
Virgin*, 1504
Pinacoteca di Brera

Francesco Guardi) and on painters exemplifying the taste for realistic representation typical of the Lombard school, such as Pitocchetto and Fra' Galgario. While the large series of paintings by Francesco Hayez dominates the rooms devoted to the 19th century, attention should also be drawn at least to the works by Giovanni Segantini, Giovanni Fattori and Silvestro Lega.

Though more modest, the section of foreign painting includes various works of merit. The museum also has two sections devoted to private collections, one housing archaeological and medieval items and modern paintings, especially 19th-century Italian works, which once belonged to Lamberto Vitali, and the other the Jesi donation. Currently exhibited in room X, this collection focuses on Italian painting from the first three decades of the 20th century, with works in particular by Medardo Rosso, Umberto Boccioni (the celebrated *Rissa in Galleria* or 'Brawl in the Gallery'), Mario Sironi, Arturo Martini, Carlo Carrà and Giorgio Morandi.

Bounded by Via Pontevetero, Via dell'Orso, Via Brera and Via Pontaccio, **Brera** is a small neighbourhood of picturesque streets lined

Francesco Hayez,
The Kiss, 1859
Pinacoteca di Brera

Umberto Boccioni,
*Brawl in the
Gallery*, 1910
Pinacoteca di Brera

The Fashion District

The *quadrilatero della moda* or Fashion district on the right at the intersection of Via Manzoni and Via Borgonuovo is a small, rich and comparatively secluded area bounded by Via della Spiga, Via Monte Napoleone and the corresponding stretch of Via Manzoni.

With its exclusive stores and boutiques designed in the minimalist and high-tech styles, this is the focal point of deluxe shopping in Milan and the showcase of a creative and productive sector that has one of its world capitals in Milan.

Fashion is the star on Via Monte Napoleone, even though there is certainly no lack of famous names in the fields of jewellery and design. The adjoining streets are characterised by a remarkable concentration of antique shops.

Via della Spiga was a sort of back street in the pre-war era. Kept very clean and tidy, it was lined with ordinary grocery stores, haberdasheries and other small shops supplying the needs of the stately mansions on the main road running parallel. Now instead, the shops of the most illustrious stylists designed by architects of international renown are located here as a setting for glamorous events.

Via Monte Napoleone as seen from Via Croce Rossa

Via della Spiga

202

with stately mansions, antique shops and clubs, and enlivened during the day by the presence of students from the academy. Apart from the Palazzo di Brera housing the Pinacoteca, the major monument is the **Church of Santa Maria del Carmine**. Located on the piazza of the same name, it was built in the 15th century using material from the destroyed Visconti Castle (the first phase in the construction of the Sforza Castle). The inevitable restoration work carried out in the 19th century involved the creation of an invented façade in Gothic-Lombard style. It has a three-aisled nave with groin vaulting and holds various works by important artists. The sumptuous Chapel of the Madonna del Carmine, to the right of the presbytery, is by Procaccini (1616–1619).

Giovanni di Balduccio, *Funeral Monument of the Blessed Lanfranco Settala*
Church of San Marco

Church of Santa Maria del Carmine, façade

The **Church of San Marco** also stands in the vicinity of Brera in the piazza of the same name. It was founded in 1254 and originally located outside the city walls. The only surviving parts of the original structure, namely the bell tower and the front of the right transept, can be seen in the rear section of the building. The façade was rebuilt in the 19th century, preserving the older entrance and the three statues above it. A large number of 16th-century paintings by members of the Lombard school can be seen in the totally Baroque interior. Two ancient frescoes depicting the *Crucifixion* and the *Assumption* were discovered in the right transept. Attention should be drawn to the sarcophagus of the Blessed Lanfranco Settala, the founder of the church, which has a bas-relief of a monk surrounded by pupils on the front and is attributed to Giovanni di Balduccio from Pisa.

We now walk a short way along Via Solferino and turn left into Via Cavalieri del Santo Sepolcro to visit the **Basilica of San Simpliciano**, which stands on the site once occupied by the ancient *Basilica Virginum* (circa 385–401), founded by Saint Ambrose and then continued by his successor Saint Simplician. The outer walls survive in the present-day church and are clearly visible along the right side,

Bergognone,
Coronation of the Virgin, circa 1515
Basilica of San Simpliciano

where we can see two tiers of blind arches. The present appearance of the basilica, with groin vaulting, octagonal dome and transept, is the result of the disastrous work carried out in the 19th century to restore it to its hypothetical Romanesque form even at the cost of damaging original parts. Again largely rebuilt in the 19th century along Neo-Romanesque lines, the façade does at least incorporate some fragments of ancient decorative elements. The concha of the apse is adorned with a large fresco by Bergognone (circa 1515) depicting the *Coronation of the Virgin* with ranks of brightly coloured angels and saints in the background.

Before taking Via Statuto and proceeding toward the Monumental Cemetery, we can make a short detour by turning right at Largo Treves and continuing as far as the Church of Sant'Angelo in the piazza of the same name (**Piazza Sant'Angelo**), where there is also a poetic fountain of *Saint Francis Preaching to the Birds* by Giannino Castiglioni (1926). Work started on the construction of the church and the adjoining Franciscan monastery in 1552, after the Order's previous complex had been demolished to make way for the new walls. While the monastery was rebuilt by Giovanni Muzio in the 20th century, the church retains its original decoration and structure intact. The austere interior flooded with light exemplifies the canons of Milan's late 16th-century religious architecture. The fresco of the *Assumption of Mary* on the triumphal arch between the end of the nave and the presbytery is the work of Legnanino.

7

Having arrived in Largo La Foppa at the end of Via Statuto, we can turn right into Corso Garibaldi to visit the **Church of Santa Maria Incoronata**, which consists of two originally separate buildings joined together in 1484.

The building of the first, which corresponds to the present-day right aisle, was ordered by Francesco Sforza in 1451. The second is similar in all respects and was constructed a few years later. The interior, which is now painted white but was originally decorated with series of paintings and frescoes, has a groin-vaulted ceiling resting on pillars and three polygonal chapels on the right side. The alternative is to take Via Volta as far as Via Ceresio, a wide tree-lined avenue built in the 19th century to provide access to the city's Monumental Cemetery.

Created by Carlo Maciachini over the period 1863–1866 and subsequently expanded, the **Monumental Cemetery** was originally a vast rectangular area surrounded by a fence. The main entrance was through the Famedio (from the Latin *famae aedes*: temple of fame), the burial place of the most illustrious citizens, and the wings stretching out on either side. Constructed with a great variety of stone and marble, the buildings make clear references to the medieval Lombard tradition, as is very common in Milan's official works of eclectic architecture. The tombs, monuments and shrines filling all the available space in the complex, through which Milan's ruling classes sought to perpetuate and celebrate their memory, constitute an authentic compendium of sculptural styles with works ranging from halfway through the 19th century up to the present day.

The cemetery includes a significant group of monumental tombs built in different styles by leading architects, such as the historicist architecture of Luca Beltrami and the Liberty style of Giuseppe Sommaruga, Ernesto Pirovano and Ulisse Stacchini.

The representatives of the Milanese architecture that developed between the two world wars, oscillating between the Novecento movement and Rationalism, include Paolo Mezzanotte, Piero Portaluppi, Gio Ponti, the BBPR group, Luigi Figini and Gino Pollini. Greater formal and thematic freedom is found in the shrines, starting with those created by Medardo Rosso (who is buried there in the non-Catholic sector in a tomb of his own design). Attention should also be drawn to Enrico Butti, whose tomb sculpture for Isabella Casati is a realistic portrayal of the deceased on her deathbed, and to Ernesto Bazzaro's sculpture of the *Raising of Lazarus* for the Squadrelli tomb. With its predilection for sophisticated figuration in a new style of greater harmony and fluidity, the language of Symbolism paved the way in the 1890s for the popularity of Art Nouveau and the Liberty style, its Italian version, which was to continue up to the end of the 1920s with the inventions of Leonardo Bistolfi and dozens of imitators. The sculptural vocabulary became less ornate in the period between the two world wars while exploring a variety of differ-

Bernocchi
Monument, detail,
1936
Monumental
Cemetery

ent avenues, from the expressive approach of Adolfo Wildt to the physicality of Carlo Bonomi. The 1940s opened with the new classicism and formal polish of Arturo Martini and Lucio Fontana. The works created in the closing decades of the 20th century include sculptures by Francesco Messina, Giacomo Manzù and Giò Pomodoro.

From Corso Garibaldi to Piazzale Maciachini: The Transformation of the Suburbs

8

We set out from Corso Garibaldi, a charming pedestrian area in the historic working-class centre of Milan, with its distinctive balconied houses. It is well worth exploring this unexpected tangle of courtyards, paths and hidden treasures. Along the first stretch of the avenue, on the right, we find the Romanesque **Basilica of San Simpliciano** (see Itinerary 7), with a wide cobbled churchyard. Overlooking the elegant cloisters – partly restored by the BBPR group in the 1930s – is the former convent, now housing the Theological University. We continue our walk with a view of the **UniCredit Tower** designed by Cesar Pelli, one of the architectural landmarks of the new Milan we are approaching.

After crossing the busy Largo La Foppa, we continue to follow the pedestrian street until on our right we find the unusual 15th-century 'double' **Church of Santa Maria Incoronata** (see Itinerary 7), commissioned by Francesco Sforza. Imposing monuments – which along Corso Garibaldi acquire an almost domestic aura through their alternation with many residential buildings from the post-war period – continue to meet our eyes all the way down to Piazza XXV Aprile and **Porta Garibaldi** (known as Porta Comasina up until 1860). One of the six main gateways to Milan, it was carved out of the **Bastioni** (city walls). At the centre stands the neoclassical arch by Giacomo Moraglia (1826–1828), flanked by two toll houses (1834). Overlooking the square is the former **Smeraldo Theatre** (designed by Ottavio Cabiati and Alessandro Rimini in 1938), now recently renovated as the **Eataly Food Centre**: an elegant example of a multifunctional building of the 1930s that combined a cinema, a theatre and residential units. From here we reach Corso Como, on the edge of the historic centre. Originally a working-class area, with charming balconied houses, today it is an elegant shopping district. This avenue leads to the Porta Nuova area, newly developed by the Hines group. A light slope, flanked by

Piazza Gae Aulenti with the UniCredit Tower

211

two yellow residential blocks designed by the Spanish firm Muñoz + Albin, descends into **Piazza Gae Aulenti**. Like the skyscraper that towers over it and the master plan for the whole area, the new square was designed by the Argentinian-American master Cesar Pelli. Past the fine golden statue by Alberto Garutti, we reach the open square, with a large basin and fountain which may be crossed at its centre. Overlooking the square are the captivating UniCredit Tower (at 230 metres in height, the tallest in Italy) and the sinuous, white building designed for ateliers and galleries by the Piuarch studio. Not far away, on the opposite side, is the curved wooden structure of the **UniCredit Pavilion** by aMDL (Michele De Lucchi) which will soon be flanked by the squared **office building and retail** designed by MC A Mario Cucinella Architects. On the side of this building, just outside the Porta Nuova area, the raised square affords a view of the **Corte Verde di Corso Como** residences by CZA (Cino Zucchi Architetti), with an irregular, faceted outline and long balconies or landings opening up onto a private garden. Redirecting our gaze towards the square and turning to face the other direction, we obtain a fascinating view: visible on the right are the new **Residential Towers** by the Spanish firm Arquitectonica (**Aria, Solaria**) and Caputo Partnership, the **Residence Porta Nuova** by Marco Zanuso and Piero Crescini (1973), renewed on a project by Park Associati, and the dark red 'villas' by M2P. Emerging in the dis-

Piazza Gae Aulenti

Piazza Gae Aulenti with Alberto Garutti's sculpture

Following pages
A view of the new Milan

tance, in the direction of Viale della Liberazione, is the **Diamond Tower** (the 'Diamantone') by Kohn Pedersen Fox, foreshadowed by the equally glass-encased two-block office building designed by the same architects. Here we also catch a glimpse of Gio Ponti's Pirelli skyscraper, the **Milan Tower** by Mattioni and Soncini, and a range of other high-rise buildings and office towers that once embodied the modern side of the city and its services district, adjacent to the Milan Central Railway Station. Gazing to the left from the skyscraper under which we are standing, beyond the street and the green area designed by the Land studio, we can make out the **Garibaldi Railway Station** (Minoletti, Tevarotto, Gentili Tedeschi, 1958–1960): once highly innovative, this steel-plated structure is surmounted by two towers renovated by Progetto CMR. A sloping pathway flanked by green stretches opens up beyond the reflecting pool. As we follow it, the two **Bosco Verticale** towers by Boeri Studio soon come into view, with their deep plant-filled balconies (hence the name of the buildings: vertical forest). On the right, overlooking Via de Castillia, are the headquarters of the **Riccardo Catella Foundation**, surrounded by a charming garden with playground structures. The restored historic building is worth visiting for the scale model that illustrates the radical transformation of the Porta Nuova area. At the end of the street stands an imposing glass-encased skyscraper known as **L'Altra Sede**, the new seat of the Lombardy regional government. Featuring ribbon-like, sinuous bands below and a split tower above, the building is the work of the American firm Pei, Cobb, Freed & Partners with Caputo Partnership. We have now

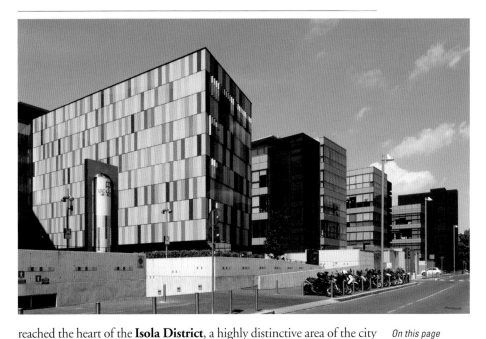

reached the heart of the **Isola District**, a highly distinctive area of the city packed with trendy bars and artisan ateliers. Here we find three of the five houses developed by the Rationalist architects Giuseppe Terragni and Pietro Lingeri in Milan between 1933 and 1935: on the corner between Via Pepe and Via Cola Montano stands the **Rustici Comolli House**; in Piazzale Lagosta, on the corner with Via Garigliano, the **Ghiringhelli House**; in Via Perasto, the **Toninello House**. Continuing along Via Perasto we reach Via Farini. Following this long street away from the city centre, we come to Piazzale Maciachini and then Via Imbonati, and move on to discover another interesting area which has been completely redeveloped in recent years: the **Former Carlo Erba Plant**, now the **Maciachini Business Park**. Aside from the slick spaces designed by Italo Rota as commercial venues and fitness areas (Virgin and Lewis branches), with their bright colours, what stands out is the system of three interconnected office buildings by the Anglo-German firm Sauerbruch Hutton, with a distinctive glass casing that reflects the nuances of colour in this historic suburb of Milan. As we make our way into the park, on the right we can see the more conventional looking administrative centre designed by Maurice Kanah, which partly incorporates some pre-existing structures. Towering beyond the large green area developed for the benefit of the whole district is the hybrid outline of the headquarters of **Zurich Assicurazioni Italia** by the Scandurrastudio. The slender, somewhat Japanese architecture of the **Food Park** designed by Paolo Pasquini — also the author of the overall plan for the area — marks the service area, the heart of the business centre.

On this page and opposite The Maciachini Business Park

Index of Places

Houses, Villas and Palazzi

223